HIGH PQ™

THE P.I.V.O.T. QUOTIENT THAT CHANGES EVERYTHING

A Blueprint for Building Resilience, Rewriting Your Story, and Leading Through Any Storm

CONSTANTINE J. ALLEYNE

High PQ™: The P.I.V.O.T. Quotient That Changes Everything
© 2025 by Constantine J. Alleyne

All rights reserved. No part of this book may be reproduced, distributed, or transmitted in any form or by any means, including photocopying, recording, or other electronic or mechanical methods, without the prior written permission of the publisher, except in the case of brief quotations embodied in critical reviews and certain other noncommercial uses permitted by copyright law. For permission requests, write to the publisher at the address below.

Published by Alleyne Publishing
Bloomfield, Connecticut, USA

ISBN: 979-8-9897909-5-1

Interior design by Honeylette Pino

This is a work of nonfiction. While every effort has been made to ensure the accuracy of information provided within, the author and publisher assume no responsibility for errors, inaccuracies, or omissions. The information contained in this book is for educational and informational purposes only and is not intended as professional advice.

Printed in the United States of America

First Edition

10 9 8 7 6 5 4 3 2 1

Dedication

To my daughter, Kendall—my north star in human form. You are the exhale after every storm, the rhythm in my stride, the fire behind my "why." Watching you rise with dignity despite the weight of a diagnosis has taught me that courage isn't always loud—sometimes, it shows up in blood sugar checks and whispered prayers in the dark.

To my mother—your hands built bridges where there were none. You taught me how to stand tall with grace when the world expected me to shrink.

To my family and dear friends, whose quiet support has been the soft place I've landed more times than I can count—thank you for loving me through every plot twist, every pivot, every leap of faith that looked like risk but was always rooted in purpose.

To the mentors, both formal and divine, who didn't just show me the path but dared me to build one of my own—thank you for holding mirrors and opening doors.

To every woman who hears the whisper but fears the weight of her calling, this book is your echo. Your permission slip. Your push. And to the allies—the ones who don't just include us in rooms but advocate when we're absent, who name us with reverence when no one's watching—you are the kind of necessary that history remembers. This isn't just a dedication. It's a love letter. A war cry. A thank you to the ones who shaped me, stood by me, and believed I could fly—even before I grew wings.

Epigraph

"You will not always be warned before you are rerouted.
The door won't always knock before it closes.
But if you listen closely—beneath the noise, beyond the fear—
there is a whisper that says: Shift.
Not because it's easy. Not because it's safe.
But because it's time."

— Constantine J. Alleyne

Contents

Foreword vii
Future-Facing Preface ix
Preface xi

PART I
THE PIVOT MINDSET – WHY WE STAY STUCK

Chapter 1:   Comfortable is a Cage 3
Chapter 2:   Permission Denied, Still Moved Anyway 10
Chapter 3:   The Myth of Linear Growth 17

PART II
THE P.I.V.O.T.™ BLUEPRINT – THE 5 MOVES THAT CHANGE EVERYTHING

Chapter 4:   P is for Pause — Power in the Stillness 27
Chapter 5:   I is for Identify — The Lesson in the Loss 36
Chapter 6:   V is for Validate — Honor It, Don't Host It 44
Chapter 7:   O is for Own — Power Looks Good on You 52
Chapter 8:   T is for Take Action — Move Without Permission 60

PART III
THE RISE – PIVOTING AS A WAY OF LIFE

Chapter 9:   Introducing *Pivot Quotient*™: The Missing Element 71
Chapter 10: The Bounce Quotient: Why Speed Outweighs Spectacle 73
Chapter 11: *The Pivot Quotient*™: Resilience Reimagined 83

Chapter 12: Shift Culture, Not Just Circumstances..90
Chapter 13: The Legacy Pivot...98

PART IV
THE INFRASTRUCTURE OF HIGH PQ™

Chapter 14: The Science of the Pivot...107
Chapter 15: *Pivot Quotient*™: How We Now Measure Resilience 115
Chapter 16: Rewriting the Future — Faith, Legacy, and the Courage to
                Imagine Beyond 122
Chapter 17: Voices That Laid the Groundwork — And Why I Chose to
                Build My Own Blueprint 129
Chapter 18: Preview What's Next..133

Conclusion..137
Acknowledgments 139
References 141
Appendix A 145

Foreword

I've had the distinct honor of witnessing Constantine Alleyne navigate her many pivots in life. While I celebrated her outward successes, I hadn't fully realized the deliberate and disciplined work behind them—work now captured in this powerful book.

In every environment that I've led, from high-stakes operations to organizational leadership, I've learned a simple truth: progress belongs to those who know how to adapt. Many of us are handed a familiar script—find stability, build a career, follow your passions. Those milestones matter. But beneath them is a quieter invitation: the call to pivot.

"The future doesn't belong to those who stand still. It belongs to those who pivot with purpose."

That call is easy to ignore. It whispers through moments of disruption, discomfort, and uncertainty. Yet, for those willing to listen, it becomes the starting point of transformation.

This is where Constantine's work stands apart. The *P.I.V.O.T.*™ framework is not just a concept—it is a practical, evidence-based system for turning adversity into advantage. Pause. Identify. Validate. Own. Take Action. These five moves offer a clear and repeatable roadmap for anyone—whether you're leading a team, running a business, or charting the next chapter of your life.

"High PQ™ is more than a metric—it's a mindset that equips leaders, creators, and changemakers to transform disruption into direction."

Personally, this book has brought language and structure to my own pivots. It clarified lessons I had lived and gave me the tools to move forward with greater confidence and purpose. Constantine's reminder—"Failure didn't break you; it introduced you to the part of success that was hidden"—is one I now hold close, not only for myself but for those I've had the privilege to lead.

To you, the reader: you've chosen the right guide. What you hold in your hands isn't just a book—it's a blueprint. Apply it, and you won't simply survive change; you'll learn how to leverage it and thrive.

Gregson Haynes, Command Master Chief, Retired United States Navy

Future-Facing Preface

The Pivot That Builds What's Next

This book is not just the story of how I pivoted—it's the blueprint for how we all build what's next.

High PQ: The P.I.V.O.T. Quotient That Changes Everything was born from rupture—unexpected losses, sacred disruptions, and systems that were not designed with our wholeness in mind. But what emerged from those moments wasn't just personal insight. It was a framework. A language. A movement.

We live in a world that demands agility but rarely teaches adaptation. That rewards performance but punishes pause. That tells us to "bounce back" without giving us tools to *recenter forward*. That's where *PQ—the Pivot Quotient*™—comes in. If IQ measures intellect and EQ measures emotional intelligence, then PQ is your resilience intelligence. It's how you move—not just through change, but because of it.

This isn't theory—it's practice.
This isn't self-help—it's self-honor.
This isn't a memoir—it's a manual for becoming.

But let me be clear: what you're holding is only the beginning.

High PQ™ is already evolving. In its next form, you'll see the emergence of *High PQ*™ *2.0*—introducing deeper metrics, cultural nuance, bio-adaptive tools, and new models of collective resilience. Because legacy doesn't just live in what you survived. It lives in what you systematize.

So read this as both a map and a mirror.
Let it prepare you. Let it provoke you.
Let it remind you that you are the experiment and the evidence.
You are not just pivoting for yourself. You are pivoting for the future that needs you.

Preface

The Pivot I Became

Before this book had a title, before it had a framework or even the faintest whisper of structure—it had a pulse. A rhythm beating beneath the surface of my life, long before I could name it. I didn't write this book because I had all the answers. I wrote it because I survived the questions.

My journey didn't begin with clarity. It began with disruption. Let's recognize that some pivots don't come from pain at all—they come from peace. My pivots came from a quiet knowing that I had outgrown my current chapter. My pivots weren't born from burnout, but from evolving brilliance. With rooms that couldn't hold me and roles that asked me to shrink. I didn't pivot once. I pivoted repeatedly. Not because I was lost—but because I was becoming.

And I know I'm not the only one.

What I didn't know then—but understand now—is that not all pivots are created equal. Each one reveals a different resilience archetype. Some rise as Architects, others as Alchemists. The *Pivot Quotient*™ became my way of making sense of those distinctions.

Whether you're a father starting over, a leader rethinking your purpose, or a woman shedding old expectations like old skin—this book was built with you in mind. It's not just a guide for career shifts or fresh starts. It's for anyone brave enough to outgrow who they were told to be.

My pivots weren't polished. They weren't linear. But they were sacred.

This book was born not in stillness, but in motion. In the gritty motion of choosing alignment over applause. It was forged in the tension between who I was expected to be and who I dared to become.

Let me take you back to the beginning—not the curated one. The real one.

I was a first-gen college grad of an immigrant mother and a Southern father whose faith and sacrifice held up our family. I grew up knowing survival was currency and gratitude was non-negotiable. Then came Wall Street. Suits, schedules, and six-figure smiles. I had arrived—or so they said. But what no one tells you is that success can be a cage wrapped in praise. I had the title but not the truth. I had the paycheck but not the pulse.

So I pivoted. And sometimes, not with ache—but with aspiration. Some of the most transformative moves I've made weren't to escape pain, but to embody potential.

I left the prestige behind to sit beside my grandmother after her triple bypass. In that sterile hospital room, I became more than her granddaughter—I became her advocate. That's where a new version of me began to emerge.

Next came betrayal—by leaders who exploited my labor and colleagues who knew better but said nothing. I quit. Again. Not out of recklessness—but out of refusal. I would not be complicit in a culture that dishonored its people.

That refusal became my freedom.

Then came Rikers Island. I didn't end up there by accident—I chose to walk into one of the most complex, heartbreaking institutions in this country as a discharge planner. I became fluent in pain, systems, and survival. I advocated for individuals with mental illness trying to re-enter a society that had already discarded them. It was in those fluorescent-lit corridors where I truly learned: leadership isn't a title. It's a vow.

From union delegate to health services manager, from director of a residential program to a domestic violence shelter—I wasn't climbing a ladder. I was excavating purpose.

I pivoted again—this time to Connecticut, with nothing but my eighteen-month-old daughter and an unshakable conviction. I became a prison health administrator. I bought a home. I enrolled in the Executive MBA program at UCONN. And eventually, I entered the world of aerospace. Because, why not?

I wasn't following a blueprint. I was becoming one.

There was no straight line. What I had was a spiral. A *Nonlinear Legacy*™—where every pivot deepened my capacity for impact.

Through it all, I said yes to God's whispers; I said yes to disruption. I said yes to my own evolution—especially when it terrified me.

And then came the pivot that rearranged my soul: my daughter Kendall's Type 1 diabetes diagnosis. That day cracked me open—but it also constructed something lasting.

PREFACE

From it came the Kendall Wyche Foundation. A mission. A new layer of me. One that no corporate title could contain.

This book is not a memoir. It's a mirror.

It's not about me—it's about what moved through me. And now, what can move through you.

Because the truth is, we are all walking contradictions. Soft and strong. Brave and breaking. We are pivots in motion.

And that's where *High PQ*™ was born.

If IQ measures intellect, and EQ measures emotion, *PQ*™—your *Pivot Quotient*™— measures your ability to recover, reimagine, and rise. It's not about bouncing back higher. It's about bouncing back faster, with intention. It's about recalibrating in real time and reclaiming your power before the dust has even settled.

The *P.I.V.O.T.*™ framework—Pause, Identify, Validate, Own, Take Action—was not developed in a lab. It was excavated in crisis. Formed in systems that weren't built for us but still demanded our performance. It's for every person who's ever had to rebuild while still bleeding. For those who had to rise before rest was an option.

And let me be clear: this book is not just for women.

It's for fathers who've lost jobs and redefined their manhood. For professionals starting over. For people rebuilding after grief, loss, or unexpected turns. It's for the overlooked, the underestimated, the mischaracterized. For the people navigating silent wars no one applauds.

This is a book for the builder. The one in transition. The one whose identity is evolving faster than the world's permission slip.

This is your permission slip.

You won't find perfection in these pages. But you will find power. Power rooted in agency, identity, and narrative reclamation. You'll find Bandura's self-efficacy, Maslow's hierarchy of needs, Crenshaw's intersectionality, Valerie Young's impostor truths—all folded into lived experience and remixed for modern transformation.

You'll find rhythm. Resistance. Rebirth.

This is *Shift Happens*, elevated. This is *High PQ*™, defined. This is legacy—rewritten.

So welcome, reader. Not to a story—but to your own revolution.

You don't need a plan to pivot. You need a pulse.
You don't need permission to evolve. You need presence.
You don't need applause. You need alignment.

You are the pivot. You are the proof.
Let's rise.

PART I

THE PIVOT MINDSET – Why We Stay Stuck

Chapter 1
COMFORTABLE IS A CAGE

Unpopular Truth: Stability can be more dangerous than failure.

Comfort has a way of convincing us it's safety, but in reality, it's often the slowest form of surrender. This chapter peels back the illusion of stability to reveal the cost of staying too long in spaces we've outgrown—professionally, emotionally, and spiritually. The purpose here is simple: to show that growth is not always in the leap, but in the courage to acknowledge when you've settled.

We glamorize comfort like it's the finish line—like if we can just get the job, the house, the partner, the title, the applause, we'll finally exhale. But here's the truth they don't put on vision boards: comfort is often just fear in expensive shoes. It's a pretty prison dressed up as prestige.

No one talks about how success can smother you. That prestige can suffocate. That the same applause that built you can also bury you.

No one warns you that it's possible to be celebrated publicly and spiritually starved. That you can cash checks and still feel bankrupt. That you can be everyone's role model and still be a stranger to yourself.

I Know This Because I Lived It

The 2 train from Brooklyn to Wall Street. Tailored suits. Elevators that spoke in numbers and names. A salary that made my mother cry tears of joy—and pride. On paper, I had "made it." But under the surface, I was unraveling.

Every morning, I put on my competence like armor. Every night, I peeled it off with exhaustion. My heartbeat was synced to deadlines, not dreams. My spirit didn't sing—it sighed. What I had once called success had slowly become sedation.

And the cruel irony? I had fought like hell to get there. I was a first-generation college student. The daughter of a Barbadian immigrant and a sharecropper's son. I believed that breaking generational cycles meant blending in, excelling, and enduring. I thought arrival was freedom.

But escape isn't the same as liberation.

Security became my sentence. The golden handcuffs? Still handcuffs. And I wore them with a smile.

The Neuroscience of Stagnation

Let's disrupt this myth with science.

Your brain isn't wired for your highest self. It's wired for your safest self. The "default mode network"—the part of your brain that lights up during self-reflection—favors routine over risk (Raichle et al., 2001). This wiring evolved to protect us from physical danger, but now it keeps us stuck in emotional and professional ruts.

Why do we stay in jobs that erode us? Why do we keep saying yes to systems that exploit us? Why do we live for weekends instead of waking up each day with excitement and purpose?

Because the brain interprets *familiarity* as *safety*. And interprets *possibility* as *threat*.

Kahneman and Tversky (1979) call this "loss aversion"—the idea that we'd rather avoid pain than pursue joy. Even if the discomfort is obvious, change often feels more threatening than misery. So we don't move. We numb.

But survival is the bare minimum. The floor. You were not created to simply manage your life. You were designed to *expand* in it.

The Reckoning

Walking away from Wall Street wasn't a slow clap moment. It wasn't a TED Talk, or a mic drop. It was a silent scream. A string of quiet rebellions. A reckoning between the version of me who had been applauded—and the version who had been silenced.

I had to admit: I didn't recognize myself.

I had confused my résumé with my worth.
I had mistaken my performance for presence.
I had let my productivity become a permission slip to ignore my pain.

Erica knows what I mean. She was a rock star in tech, commanding six figures and a team. But at night, she couldn't sleep. Her soul ached. So she walked away and built a wellness collective rooted in ancestral healing. "I was securing everyone else's bag while bankrupting my own soul," she told me.

Luis knows, too. He was expected to inherit the family business. Instead, he got a Master's in Social Work and founded a trauma center for young men of color. "I needed to sell healing, not hardware," he said. His pivot wasn't betrayal. It was liberation.

And then there's Marcus, a mid-level sales director who, after a quiet layoff, turned his love for sneakers into a multi-platform sneaker restoration business. No MBA. Just motivation. His pivot wasn't loud, but it was liberating.

These aren't tales of rebellion. They're blueprints for reclamation.

Choosing Expansion Over Expectation

Here's the quiet revolution: *Not every pivot begins with a plan. Some begin with a holy unrest.* Some pivots aren't loud or laced with loss. They emerge gently—from a nudge, a whisper, a sacred discomfort. Not all pivots are reactions. Some are revolutions led by alignment.

A whisper that says, "This ain't it."
A lump in your throat you can't swallow anymore.
A question that won't leave you alone: *What if there's more?*

This is the first step in the ***P.I.V.O.T.*** ™ **framework**:
P – Pause. You don't need a ten-year strategy. You
need a ten-second moment of honesty.

Your comfort zone will convince you that stagnation is stability. That burnout is just the cost of ambition. That survival is the ceiling.

But fear is not your enemy.

Staying stuck is.

Your Turn to Shift

Reflect:

- Where in your life have you mistaken *comfort* for *calling*?
- What part of your daily routine feels like a performance instead of purpose?
- Who are you shrinking for—and why?

Now write a letter to your future self. The version of you who chose alignment over applause. Who stopped playing small to keep others comfortable. Who walked away from the cage, even when the cage came with benefits.

Thank her. Then become her.

Shift Snapshot: Devon, The Nurse Who Became a Founder

Devon was an ICU nurse. Brilliant. Burned out. When COVID hit, her hospital became a war zone. And yet, she kept showing up. Until she couldn't.

She took a pause. A breath. Then she pivoted. No MBA. No tech experience. Just conviction. She built a mental health startup for frontline workers and is now pitching to VCs.

Devon didn't wait for permission. She followed her pain into purpose.

Her pivot wasn't perfect. But it was powerful.

Chapter Takeaway

- A pivot isn't just a change in direction—it's a conscious recalibration of identity, purpose, and alignment.
- Every pivot begins with disruption. Don't fear it—interrogate it. Disruption is your compass.

What I didn't realize then—but understand now—is that not all pivots are the same. Some are protective. Others prophetic. That distinction would later fuel the creation of the *PQ Matrix*™—a visual language for decoding how we adapt.

You've survived the impact. Now it's time to decode the pattern. What if growth doesn't come in a straight line—but in a sacred swirl? Let's debunk the myth of linear success.

Figure 1.1 – *Mirror Moment™* Reflection Tool

Figure 1.1: The Mirror Moment™ *is designed to create space for your internal truth to surface—before you take action, set goals, or seek applause. Use this as a private reflection or in tandem with the* Inner Voice Rewrite™.

Mirror Moment™

Your space to reflect, reveal, and realign.

Chapter 2
PERMISSION DENIED, STILL MOVED ANYWAY

Unpopular Truth: Most of the gates keeping you out were built by people who never intended to let you in.

Sometimes the most defining pivot doesn't come from inspiration, but rejection. Being told you don't belong can either shrink your spirit or spark your shift. This chapter explores the power of moving without permission, anchored in the belief that boundaries built by others are often broken by purpose.

You were never supposed to make it here.

Not to this boardroom.

Not to this mic.

Not to this moment.

You weren't groomed for greatness; you were groomed for gratitude. Be thankful. Be small. Be quiet.

And for a while—you complied. You wore gratitude like armor, shrinking your light just enough to be palatable. You learned how to soften your voice in rooms that didn't know how to hold your power. Until one day, something shifted.

You stopped asking to be chosen.

Because here's what no one tells you: some of the most radical pivots don't start with passion. They begin with rejection. A door closed. A voice silenced. A dream delayed. Not because it was unworthy, but because it was unwelcomed.

This chapter is for every leader, every creator, every bold soul whose pivot began with a firm no—and a deeper knowing.

The Invisible Rules

Gatekeeping doesn't always look like a slammed door. Sometimes it's a smile with strings attached:

"You're too ambitious."
"Wait your turn."
"Be a team player."
"Let someone else go first."

Sometimes it's written into handbooks. Sometimes it's whispered in interviews. And sometimes, it's etched deep into your nervous system—coded through generational trauma and social scripts.

Imposter syndrome thrives in environments where authenticity is penalized, and assimilation is praised. But it's not just a mindset issue—it's a structural consequence. As Dr. Valerie Young (2011) reminds us, high-achieving women, especially from marginalized backgrounds, often internalize the idea that they're frauds in spaces never built with them in mind. Kimberlé Crenshaw's (1991) intersectionality theory goes further—showing us how race, gender, class, and identity do not exist in silos, but collide at dangerous intersections creating unique experiences of discrimination and social inequality.

And those collisions? They cause cultural bruises we're taught to cover with professionalism.

My Gate Was Made of Glass

There was a day—a crackling, unforgettable day—when I realized I had internalized someone else's ceiling as my sky.

I had been told—again—to "wait my turn."
Again?

I had waited through condescension dressed as mentorship. Waited while others, with lighter skin and louder mediocrity, leapfrogged into leadership. Waited while doing the work, holding the line, making it look easy.

Until I finally said what my soul had been screaming:

The gate isn't closed because I'm unqualified. It's closed because it wasn't meant to open for people like me.

And so—I built my own.

Because the truth is, the same voice that was once silenced can become the voice that shakes systems.

The Unapplauded Pivots

Let's talk about what it really looks like to move without permission.

- Nia, a tenured professor, published groundbreaking research on Black maternal health. She was denied tenure for "cultural misalignment." She left. She now leads a global nonprofit that influences health policy across five continents.
- Andre, a corporate executive who chaired five diversity councils and doubled profits, was labeled "too political." He walked away. Today, he shapes ESG strategy for Fortune 100 companies.
- Fatima, a Middle Eastern creative director, won a national design award but was passed over for promotion. Why? Her "presence" wasn't "refined." She launched her own agency. It now outpaces her old firm.

None of them waited for permission.
None of them apologized for choosing freedom.
None of them looked back.

The Psychology of Belonging

Maslow (1943) taught us that after safety, we crave belonging. But what if every space demands that you leave pieces of yourself at the door?

What if "fitting in" means breaking off sacred parts of your identity?

In those moments, disruption becomes your only path to wholeness.

Albert Bandura's (1997) theory of self-efficacy tells us that belief in our ability to act is shaped by mastery experiences. But here's the dilemma: in systems designed to marginalize, many never get that first chance to win—to believe.

Still, we move. Despite exclusion. Despite erasure. We move.

We move not because we are ready—but because we refuse to rot in rooms that don't recognize our worth.

The *Nonlinear Legacy*™

Legacy is not always a straight line. It's not built in boardrooms or measured in metrics. It's crafted in the detours—those ragged, sacred pivots that no one clapped for.

This is ***Nonlinear Legacy Building***™: refusing to measure your life by ladders you were never meant to climb. This *Nonlinear Legacy Building*™ is the conscious act of disrupting generational expectations, realigning with purpose, and rewriting what it means to lead across seasons, not ladders.

It's building your table from the ashes of closed doors. It's becoming the person your younger self needed, and your future self will thank. It's saying: I didn't follow a blueprint. I became the architect.

Resolution: Move Without Permission

Let me speak this plainly:

You do not need permission to pivot. Not from your job. Not from your family. Not from the imaginary panel of critics in your mind.

Your pivot is not a protest.
It's a prophecy.

When I pivoted—from corrections to aerospace, from corporate to advocacy—no one rolled out a carpet. But I didn't wait. I moved anyway.

Because I've learned:
Calling doesn't require confirmation.
Liberation doesn't need a LinkedIn endorsement.
Courage is the only credential you need.

Tools for the Bold: Micro-Actions for the Permissionless

Use these journal prompts and actions to activate your unapologetic pivot:

Journal Prompts

- Whose voice is the loudest in your hesitation?
- What would you attempt if no one could say no?
- What story of rejection are you ready to rewrite?

Micro-Actions

- Email the mentor you've been afraid to reach out to.
- Launch the Instagram page for that idea you keep sitting on.
- Decline the meeting that drains your energy.
- Speak up, even if your voice shakes.

Every small step you take rewires your belief. And belief? Belief is a wrecking ball to systems that say you must wait.

Shift Snapshot: From Janitor to Justice Advocate

Jamal started as a janitor at a law firm. At night, he studied in secret—law books, case files, civil rights theory. After ten years of working his way through paralegal training, he passed the bar exam.

Today, he runs a pro bono legal clinic for men reentering society after incarceration.

He said: "I didn't just clean floors. I studied the systems that made people disappear. And then I came back with a key."

That's what happens when you pivot without permission.

Your Turn to Shift

Speak this aloud. Write it. Frame it.
Breathe it into your bones:

"I do not need permission to become.
I do not owe comfort to those who confined me.
I do not wait for gates to open.
I build my life from bricks they tried to block me with."

Chapter Takeaway

- Most barriers are not about your ability—they're about outdated systems built without you in mind.
- You don't need permission to pivot; you need clarity and conviction.

You've been waiting for someone to say it's your time. This is it.

HIGH PQ™

Mirror Moment™

Your space to reflect, reveal, and realign.

Chapter 3
THE MYTH OF LINEAR GROWTH

Unpopular Truth: Legacy isn't a ladder—it's a spiral staircase.

We've been sold a myth that success should follow a straight line. But growth rarely honors geometry—it spirals, it loops, it redirects. This chapter introduces the idea that legacies aren't built in straight lines but through nonlinear turns of resilience, recovery, and rebirth.

There's a blueprint many of us are handed from the beginning. Go to school. Get the job. Climb the ladder. Buy the house. Keep your head down. Retire comfortably.

This story sounds logical. It's orderly. Predictable. Safe.

And for some, it even works. But for the rest of us—for the firsts, the disruptors, the Black women, the cycle breakers, the dreamers born in chaos and raised on grit—the blueprint rarely fits.

Linear growth is a myth.

A beautifully marketed, socially sanctioned myth that serves those already in power and often gaslights the rest of us into thinking we're broken because we zigged when life told us to zag.

But here's the thing:

You are not behind. You are becoming.

You are not off track. You are building a track that didn't exist before you. Your journey is not linear because your purpose isn't either.

The Spiral Staircase: Rewriting the Blueprint

Growth is not a ladder—it's a spiral staircase.

You may revisit the same lessons, the same fears, the same heartbreaks. But each time, you return with new perspective. You're higher up. Stronger. Wiser. Louder.

This spiral model of transformation is the *architecture of the pivot.*

It rejects the idea that success is sequential.
It honors the truth that we often grow in cycles—through
return, reimagination, and radical revision.

This is *Nonlinear Legacy Building*™.
Not building up. Building *through.*
Not chasing the title. Chasing the truth.

It's a model that reflects the lives of people who were never invited into boardrooms but built tables anyway.
It's for those who have pivoted from Wall Street to caregiving, from corrections to aerospace, from grief to purpose.

When the Ladder Collapses

I used to think success would feel linear. That each role would perfectly prepare me for the next. That each accomplishment would make the climb smoother. But that's not what happened.

When my daughter was diagnosed with Type 1 diabetes, the ladder collapsed.
I had the title, the salary, the strategy. But none of it could hold me as a mother watching her child suffer. None of it prepared me to pause, reorient, and rebuild—not for applause, but for alignment.

That moment didn't fit the career map.
It wasn't a promotion. It wasn't a pivot you brag about on LinkedIn.

But it was a divine redirection.
It was the moment I stopped climbing and started becoming.

Nonlinear Legacy™ in Real Life

Let's talk about some legacy-builders whose journeys zigzagged.

Ava DuVernay didn't pick up a camera until her thirties. She pivoted from publicity to filmmaking with no formal training. Her legacy wasn't born from early mastery—it emerged from late permission.

Viola Davis didn't get leading roles until she was over forty. Her rise wasn't rapid, but her impact? Unmatched.

Rich Paul, from inner-city Cleveland to billion-dollar agency owner—his pivot wasn't born in a business school but in a barbershop and a belief that relationships could be currency.

We don't need more perfection arcs.
We need more permission to evolve without apology.

P is for Pause: *Stillness as Strategic Defiance*

The first step in the *P.I.V.O.T.*™ framework is Pause—and in the context of nonlinear growth, pause is more than reflection. It's rebellion.

In a world obsessed with acceleration, choosing stillness is an act of clarity.
It's saying: I refuse to keep climbing a ladder that leads
to someone else's definition of worth.

Pausing doesn't mean you're stuck.
It means you're choosing to shift on purpose—not panic.

I is for Identify: *Recognizing the Spiral*

To Identify is to name the old narrative that told you success had to be linear—and then write a new one.

Start here:
What did you once believe you'd be by twenty-five? By thirty-five?
What timelines have you outgrown?
What metrics no longer match your mission?

V is for Validate: *The Power of Your Becoming*

It's easy to shame yourself for backtracking.
To say, *"I should've been further by now."*

But what if we reframe the so-called setbacks as spiritual stretching?

What if returning to an old passion, leaving a six-figure role, going back to school, or starting from scratch wasn't regression—but refinement?

Validate the detours.
They're often divine.

O is for Own: *Building Legacy in Layers*

To Own your nonlinear story is to stop editing out the complexity for the comfort of others.

You're not just a professional. You're a mother, daughter, partner, entrepreneur, artist, healer, builder. And each of those identities doesn't replace the others—they *layer*.

Legacy isn't a single impact.
It's the accumulation of layered pivots, woven into infrastructure that outlives you.

So, build the thing.
Start the foundation.
Seed the scholarship.
Teach the next girl how to bend the rules instead of
break herself trying to follow them.

T is for Take Action: *Nonlinear Doesn't Mean Passive*

Here's the trap: thinking that nonlinear means *waiting*.

It doesn't.

Nonlinear growth still demands movement—just not movement that's always up, always loud, always celebrated.

Sometimes the most powerful action is quitting.
Or resting. Or whispering no.

Sometimes it's launching a new idea without a business plan. Sometimes it's going public with a story that once brought you shame.

You're not stalling. You're shaping.

Tool: *Your Spiral Timeline*™

Let's map the pivots that shaped you.

1. Revisit: Write down three times in your life when you felt "off-track."
2. Reframe: What did each moment *actually* give you? Skill? Clarity? Courage?
3. Return: How do you see the same themes cycling back now—but with wisdom?

You'll likely find that the same truths keep meeting you—only now, you're strong enough to hold them.

Shift Snapshot: Building Legacy Without a Ladder

Meet Layla. She was an administrative assistant for twelve years. Every time she tried to get promoted, she was told she needed "more polish."

So, she stopped asking. She started freelancing on nights and weekends. She taught herself web design. She built a client base through DMs and referrals.

At forty-two, she left her job. At forty-three, she bought her first commercial property. At forty-five, she hired her old boss to consult on *her* team.

Layla's legacy wasn't linear. But it was limitless.

Final Word: The Pivot is the Point

Let's end here:

You will not always move forward. Sometimes you will move inward. Sometimes you will loop back. Sometimes you will crumble—and then emerge as something you never imagined.

That's not failure. That's the sacred spiral of becoming.

You are not off track. You are on assignment. You are not late. You are in alignment. And when the world tries to hand you a ladder, remember:

You weren't born to climb in someone else's direction.
You were born to build, in your own rhythm, your
own language, and your own legacy.

So keep turning. Keep becoming. Keep rising—one spiral at a time. Because this journey? This messy, nonlinear, sacred, audacious journey?

It's not just yours. It's your children's blueprint.
Your community's shift.
Your ancestors' answered prayer.

Welcome to *Nonlinear Legacy Building*™.
Now let's spiral higher.

Chapter Takeaways

- Growth doesn't follow a straight line—it loops, bends, and circles back to move forward.
- *Nonlinear Legacy Building*™ honors the journey, not just the destination.

Figure 3.1 – The *P.I.V.O.T.*™ Framework Visual

P.I.V.O.T. Framework

P — **PAUSE**
Awareness before action; breaking autopilot cycles

I — **IDENTIFY**
Patterns, pain points, and internalized narratives

V — **VALIDATE**
Honoring your truth without shame or apology

O — **OWN**
Radical responsibility and agency

T — **TAKE ACTION**
Aligned micro-decisions that build momentum

Figure 3.1: The P.I.V.O.T.™ *framework guides readers through five essential phases of reinvention—Pause, Identify, Validate, Own, and Take Action—each one deepening resilience and reclaiming identity.*

Mirror Moment™

Your space to reflect, reveal, and realign.

PART II

THE P.I.V.O.T.™ BLUEPRINT – The 5 Moves That Change Everything

Chapter 4

P IS FOR PAUSE — POWER IN THE STILLNESS

Unpopular Truth: Busyness is often a socially accepted form of avoidance.

In a world wired for acceleration, choosing stillness is a radical act. But the greatest breakthroughs often begin in the pause. This chapter makes the case that stopping is not a sign of weakness—it's a strategy of power, clarity, and alignment.

We live in a world addicted to movement. Obsessed with velocity. Trained to worship the hustle, the title, the grind, the grind, the grind.

Pause? That's for the weak. For the idle. For the unambitious.
Or so they've told us.

We glorify the 5AM club, idolize the booked-and-busy lifestyle, and wear burnout like it's a badge of honor. But here's the quiet rebellion, the truth that trembles beneath all that motion:

Stillness is not the absence of power. It is the source of it.

When Life Won't Let You Move

I didn't choose my first true pause. It ambushed me.

I was mid-transition—professionally competent, personally crumbling. A strategist with no strategy. A mother in mourning, not of a life lost, but of a life redefined. My daughter's diagnosis with Type 1 diabetes shattered every illusion of certainty I had ever clung to.

Still, I tried to push through it. Tried to plan my way back to control. But you can't spreadsheet your way through grief.

Burnout doesn't knock politely. It barges in and unplugs everything. And when the world I knew went silent, I heard the only voice that mattered:

"Be still."

The Silent Terror of Stillness

Stillness doesn't scare us because it's empty. It scares us because it's honest. Because in stillness, we can no longer hide behind busy. In stillness, we meet ourselves—and sometimes, we don't like what we see.

What do you hear when the notifications stop?
What surfaces when you stop running?

The silence may reveal the truth you've worked so hard to mute:
That you're succeeding at something you no longer want. That you've outgrown the title you fought to earn.
That your rhythm is no longer your own.

Neuroscience Doesn't Lie: The Power of the Pause

Your brain is not built for constant input. The *prefrontal cortex*—the area responsible for decision-making, insight, and emotional regulation—activates most efficiently in periods of rest and reflection (Immordino-Yang et al., 2012).

Translation?
You need pause to make sense of your purpose.

What we call procrastination is often just an exhausted brain screaming for silence.

Stillness isn't a setback. It's system maintenance.

According to Baumeister et al. (1998), *decision fatigue*—the degradation of decision quality due to mental overload—sets in when we push forward without intentional breaks. That's why we make terrible choices when we're tired and impulsive.

Stillness, then, isn't weakness. IT'S WISDOM.

When Simone Biles Chose Stillness

Let's talk about a moment that stopped the world.

At the 2020 Olympics, Simone Biles—the most decorated gymnast of all time—chose not to compete. Not due to injury. But due to mental overload.

She paused.

And the world, conditioned to demand performance over personhood, didn't know how to respond.

But many of us did. Especially Black women.

Because we know what it's like to twirl for everyone else until our bodies collapse. We know the cost of pushing past the point of no return—just to meet someone else's expectations.

Simone didn't quit. She *claimed*.
She claimed her humanity in a system that profits from her superhuman output.

Her stillness was a sermon.
And we were listening.

The *P.I.V.O.T.*™ Lens: Pause as Power

Let's root this in our transformational framework.

- P is for Pause — the first, and often most ignored, step in the *P.I.V.O.T.*™ journey.
- Pause is not paralysis.
- Pause is presence.
- Pause is the point at which we stop reacting and start *remembering* who we are.

It is in the pause that we confront our internalized urgency, inherited expectations, and unresolved grief.

It is in the pause that we reclaim our right to move *intentionally* rather than *incessantly*.

Intentional Inaction: A Revolutionary Act

Psychologist John Anderson (2003) coined the term *intentional inaction*—a strategic choice to withhold action in order to preserve clarity.

Think about that.
Not every "no" is resistance.
Sometimes it's redirection.

In fact, Harvard researchers Bazerman & Tenbrunsel (2011) found that ethical lapses in leadership occur most often when leaders are rushed. Without pause, reflection disappears—and so does moral clarity.

So, what if pausing isn't passive?
What if it's prophetic?

Real-Life Parallel: The Silent CEO

Meet James.
A titan of industry. A name in every boardroom. Until a cardiac scare forced him into a sabbatical. The first month? Panic. The second? Permission.

He journaled.
He sat with his regrets.
He listened to the silence he had drowned out for years.

When he returned, he changed everything.
Shorter meetings. Built-in reflection time. An annual mental health stipend for staff. Meditation rooms in every office.

He didn't return less driven. He returned *more directed*.

James didn't lose his edge.
He found his essence.

Tool: The Pause Map™

Let's not romanticize reflection. Let's operationalize it.

Here's a tool I created during my own collapse and resurrection. It's a three-part scan to recenter you in moments of overwhelm:

The *Pause Map*™

1. Body
    - Where am I holding tension?
    - What is my body asking me to notice?
2. Belief
    - What narrative is looping in my mind right now?
    - Is it rooted in truth or trauma?
3. Becoming
    - Who am I becoming if I stay on this current path?
    - What does my future self need me to shift?

Write it down. Reread it out loud.
Let your body, belief, and becoming guide your next move—not just your fear.

Figure 4.1 – *Pause Map™* **Guide**

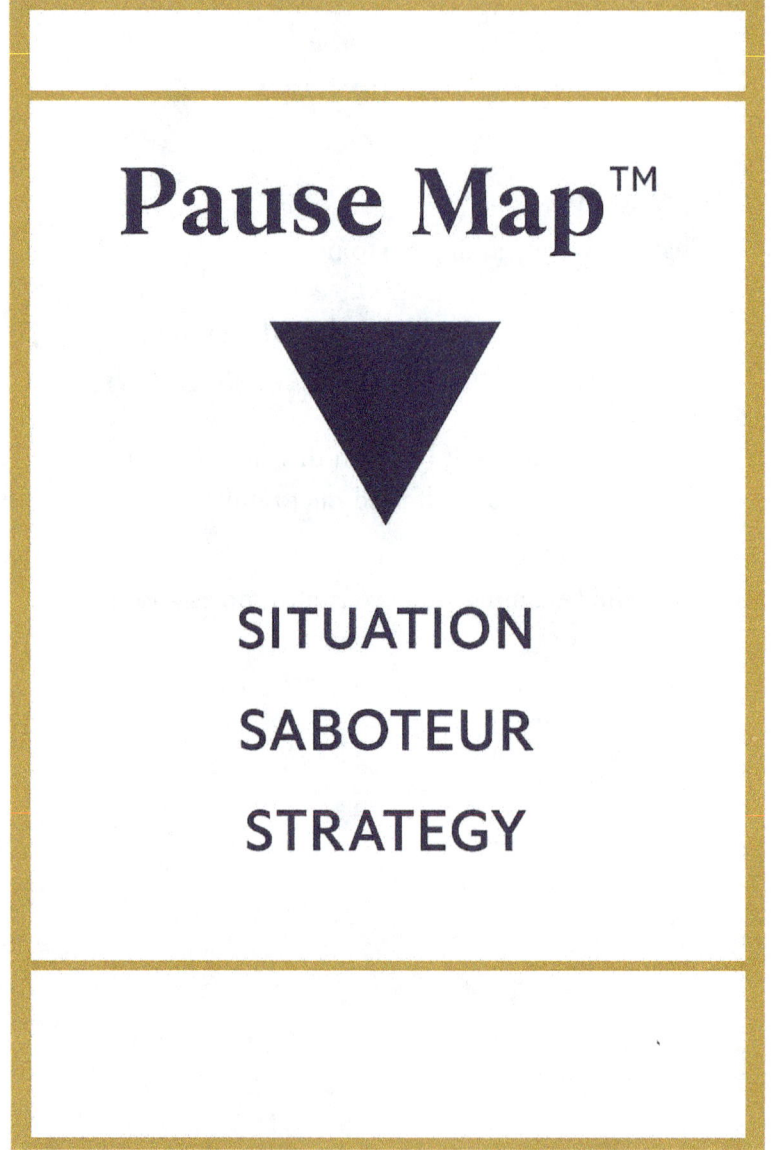

Figure 4.1: The Pause Map™ *is used to shift from reactivity to reflection. This tool is the first stop on the journey from autopilot to awareness.*

Shift Snapshot: The Silent Founder

Dalia was running a seven-figure coaching business. From the outside, she was a marvel. But inside, she was unraveling. Her pause? A digital detox. Ninety days. No social media. No client meetings.

She painted.
She wept.
She reconnected with her teenage daughter, who had
begun to mimic her burnout patterns.

When Dalia returned, she restructured her business around *seasonal flow*. Spring and Fall? Full throttle. Summer and Winter? Slowed-down strategy.

Revenue didn't dip.
But her peace? It skyrocketed.

Because when you lead from overflow—not overwork—your pivot sustains *you*, not just your output.

Your Turn to Shift

Ask yourself:

- What truth has the noise been drowning out?
- What would slowing down make room for?
- Where is God—or your gut—inviting you to *be still*?

Don't just reflect. Respond.
Block time. Shut off notifications.
Sit in silence. Sit in grace. Sit in the presence of your becoming.

Stillness will move you further than striving ever could.

It will take you inward. And *inward* is where the answers live. Busyness might impress people. But stillness? Stillness *transforms* you.

So, *pause*. Not because you're weak. But because you're wise. The shift doesn't begin with the sprint. It begins with the silence.

And in that silence, you will hear the whisper:
This is not the end. This is the alignment.

What you identify in the silence might just redirect your entire trajectory.

Chapter Takeaway

- Pause isn't weakness—it's wisdom. It's the sacred discipline of re-centering before the next leap.
- Stillness creates the clarity necessary for strategy, purpose, and powerful pivots.

Mirror Moment™

Your space to reflect, reveal, and realign.

Chapter 5

I IS FOR IDENTIFY — THE LESSON IN THE LOSS

Unpopular Truth: Your failure didn't break you. It introduced you to the part of you that success kept hidden.

Loss doesn't just strip us—it shapes us. The moments we try to forget often contain the truth we most need to confront. This chapter invites you to mine the lesson from the loss, not to romanticize pain, but to honor the identity forged in its fire.

Loss doesn't arrive with permission. It storms in.
Uninvited. Unrelenting. Unavoidable.
It kicks the door off the hinges and sits at the head
of the table, demanding to be seen.

But here's what we're rarely taught in classrooms, boardrooms, or even therapy rooms:

Loss is not just a thief. Loss is a teacher.
And sometimes, the greatest revelations don't arrive in our wins—
they're buried in the rubble of what we tried to forget.

In our world of curated triumphs and algorithm-approved joy, we rush to repackage pain into productivity. We don't just avoid our wounds. We rebrand them.

But transformation doesn't start with a reframe. It starts with *recognition*. With naming the thing we're still grieving.

That's what *Identify* means. The "I" in *P.I.V.O.T.*™ isn't about intellectualizing your pain.
It's about honoring it.

My Daughter's Diagnosis: The Identity I Didn't Choose

My most profound pivot didn't begin with a business plan. It began with a blood sugar reading of 471.

Kendall's Type 1 diabetes diagnosis detonated my sense of control. I couldn't logic my way out. Couldn't out-pray it. Couldn't out-strategize it. I was a healthcare professional, a public health expert, a mother with a binder of emergency protocols—and still, I was powerless.

I didn't just lose a sense of normalcy. I lost the illusion that I was in charge. I grieved the identity of the mother I thought I would be. I grieved the childhood I couldn't give her. I grieved *me*—the version of myself who had been taught that control was competence.

In the chaos, I met someone new:
A woman who could lead while limping.
Who could build while breaking.
Who didn't need to be certain to be strong.

Loss stripped me. But in the stripping, it revealed what success had hidden.
My soul. My softness. My truth.

What We Miss When We Skip the Mirror

We've been taught to treat loss as a detour. As failure. As weakness.
But what if loss is feedback?

Tedeschi and Calhoun (2004) introduced the idea of *Post-Traumatic Growth*—the possibility that psychological struggle can be a catalyst for profound personal development.

This isn't about toxic positivity. This isn't a "look on the bright side" slogan. It's the sacred belief that something beautiful can grow in the cracks. But, only if you're brave enough to name the cracks.

We cannot alchemize what we won't acknowledge.

As Dr. Aaron Beck (1976) emphasized in cognitive therapy that reframing can only happen *after* we face the original frame. You can't rewrite the story if you keep skipping the most painful chapter.

Identify the loss.
Don't rush it.
Don't rush yourself.

Real-Life Parallel: The Athlete Who Lost Everything (And Found Himself)

Let's talk about Derrick Rose. Youngest MVP in NBA history. Then injury. Then headlines. Then silence.

The world said, "He's finished."

But Rose didn't just rehab his body—he rehabbed his identity. "I had to fall in love with the game again," he once said. Not as a celebrity. Not as a brand. But as a *student*.

He pivoted. Not back to where he was—
But toward who he was becoming.

Or Serena Williams.

After motherhood, injury, and media crucifixion, she didn't retreat—she *expanded*. She became a venture capitalist, a fashion mogul, a truth-teller.

She didn't bounce back.
She *transcended*.

They didn't just recover. They *reclaimed*. And so can you.

Loss Is Not Always Loud

Some losses arrive with funerals. Others arrive in board meetings, bedrooms, or broken friendships. Some sound like layoffs. Others sound like, "I'm not in love anymore."

And the hardest ones? They don't make a sound at all.

They live quietly in the corners of our ambition, haunting our calendars, coloring our confidence.

But just because no one else attended the funeral doesn't mean the grief isn't real.

From Setback to Setup: A Framework for Transformation

To make sense of the mess, I created a tool.
A guide. A lifeline.

I call it the *Setback-to-Setup Timeline*™—a simple but sacred exercise in making meaning from loss.

The *Setback-to-Setup Timeline*™:

1. Name the Loss
   What changed? What ended? What didn't go the way you planned?
2. Feel the Fallout
   What emotions emerged? What identities were threatened or lost?
3. Spot the Shift
   What new insight, direction, or strength began to surface?
4. Own the Outcome
   How has this experience changed how you show up in the world?

Use this tool with brutal honesty and infinite compassion. You'll see it.
Your pivot wasn't born from progress. What was it born from?

Figure 5.1 – Timeline Visualization Tool

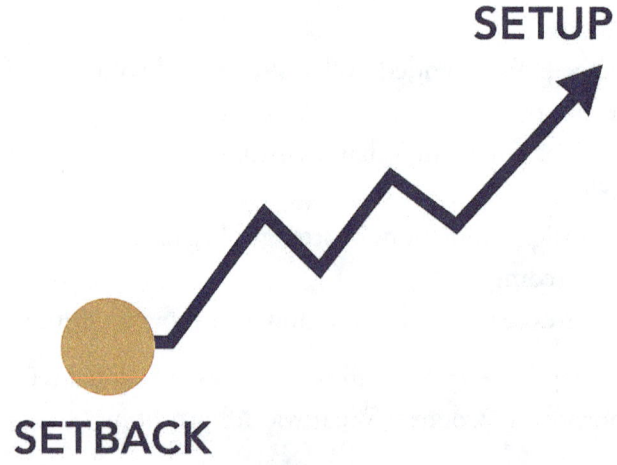

Figure 5.1: This timeline allows you to plot past setbacks and extract the set-up they created. Every loss holds the seed of a future pivot.

From Grief to Calling: Maya's Story

Maya was a powerhouse litigator. Ivy League degrees. Corner office. Killer instincts. Then came the merger. The layoff. The ego blow.

She wept for three months. She hiked. She journaled.
And in those journal pages, something stirred.

She began publishing essays on identity loss.
The essays became a blog.
The blog became a book.
The book became a *business*.

Now, Maya coaches other women through career grief.
She doesn't just help them land jobs.
She helps them reclaim *voice*.

"The layoff wasn't the end," she said.
"It was the beginning of me."

The *P.I.V.O.T.*™ Lens: Why Identify Matters

Let's bring this home:
- P is for Pause — the stillness.
- I is for Identify — the naming.

You can't move what you won't name.
You can't heal what you pretend doesn't hurt.
You can't pivot until you know *from where* you're pivoting.

Identifying the loss is not about glorifying pain.
It's about grounding your pivot in *truth*.
In data.
In depth.

Your Turn to Shift

Time to write.
Time to witness your own becoming.

Ask yourself:

- What have I lost that I've never fully grieved?
- What identity am I clinging to that no longer fits?
- What possibility has this loss created space for?

Now complete this sentence as many times as you need:

"Losing _____ taught me to find _____."

Fill it. Speak it. Feel it. Repeat until the words stop sounding like grief and start sounding like grace.

You've named the ache. You've seen the wound. Now let's honor the emotion beneath it—without letting it take the mic.

Chapter Takeaway

- Loss is a teacher in disguise. It doesn't just take—it teaches.
- To transform your pain, you must first name it.

I IS FOR IDENTIFY — THE LESSON IN THE LOSS

Mirror Moment™

Your space to reflect, reveal, and realign.

Chapter 6

V IS FOR VALIDATE — HONOR IT, DON'T HOST IT

Unpopular Truth: You can't heal what you won't feel.

Real strength isn't in silence—it's in self-honesty. Validation isn't weakness; it's wisdom. This chapter is your permission slip to feel fully, reflect honestly, and release what no longer serves you so you can move forward with intentionality and dignity.

We live in a culture that teaches us to worship productivity but grieve in private. Hustle is praised. Healing is hidden. We are hashtag #resilient but never post what it cost us.

Strength is rewarded—so long as it's stoic. But here's the deeper truth: unacknowledged pain doesn't disappear. It embeds. It echoes. It hijacks the narrative you tell about yourself.

And without validation, you don't evolve—you perform.

The Moment I Broke—And Didn't Hide It

I still remember the night Kendall's blood sugar dropped so low I thought I might lose her. My daughter. My everything. She was trembling in my arms, pale, and just a step above unresponsive. I was part mother, part medic, fully terrified. I had nothing left but adrenaline and prayer—and both were running out.

By dawn, she stabilized. But I didn't.

That morning, I made breakfast. I answered emails. I performed "okay." But inside, I was unraveling. Quietly. Elegantly. Devastatingly.

Later, standing in the bathroom mirror, I whispered, *"Why do I only allow myself to feel when no one is watching?"*

The answer: because somewhere along the way, I'd internalized the lie that vulnerability was a liability. That feelings made me fragile. That tears were unprofessional. That soft made me less strategic.

But suppression isn't strength. And avoidance isn't adaptation.

What We Silence Will Soften Our Edges

We confuse emotional control with emotional intelligence. But true emotional intelligence, as Daniel Goleman (1995) defines it, isn't about muting your feelings—it's about recognizing, understanding, and managing them with clarity and compassion.

Emotional agility, a term from Dr. Susan David (2016), takes it further. Emotions aren't threats. They're data. They aren't directives—but they are signals. And when we ignore those signals? They reroute, resurface, and sabotage.

Unchecked grief becomes reactivity. Shame masks itself as perfectionism. Anger hides beneath leadership burnout. Avoidance wears the costume of overachievement.

We suppress. We soldier on. We "lead" while leaking.

Shame Sounds Like This:

- "You're too emotional."
- "You should be over it by now."
- "Other people have it worse."

So instead of feeling our way forward, we intellectualize the pain. We overanalyze, overachieve, and under-heal.

But here's the truth you may need today:

What you won't validate will eventually violate your vision.

You cannot skip to transformation without traveling through truth. Feelings aren't flaws. They're flags. They point to unmet needs, unresolved wounds, and real-time wisdom.

The Science of Validation

In psychological research, emotional validation is the practice of recognizing and accepting your emotions as understandable and real (Linehan, 1993). It doesn't mean you agree with the feeling—it means you respect its presence.

When you validate yourself, you increase emotional regulation, reduce stress, and become more resilient over time (Shenk & Fruzzetti, 2011).

Think of emotions like guests. Some arrive with gifts. Some bring baggage. But none should be ignored at the door. Because the ones you pretend aren't there? They overstay their welcome. Quietly. Subversively.

Real-Life Parallel: Ravi's Retreat

Ravi, a nonprofit director and first-generation immigrant, spent his life performing perfection. High-functioning. Sharp. Stoic.

When his father died, he worked the next day.

During a staff retreat months later, mid-presentation—he broke. Mid-sentence, his voice cracked. Then silence. Then tears. Then applause.

"I thought my armor was protecting them," he later told me. "But it was blocking them. That day, I became more accessible. More real."

His vulnerability didn't weaken his authority. It deepened it.

Validate, But Don't Host It

Here's where the *P.I.V.O.T.*™ framework meets emotional evolution:

- Pause – When hard feelings arise, don't sprint to solve. Stop. Breathe. Acknowledge.
- Identify – What emotion is really present beneath the behavior? Is it fear masked as anger? Is it grief disguised as numbness?
- Validate – Can I allow this emotion to exist without rushing to fix or flee?
- Own – What part of this is mine to carry—and what part is a story I was taught?
- Take Action – What's one small move I can take toward healing, not hiding?

You can honor what you feel without handing it the mic. Emotions need a seat—not the stage.

Parenting, Partnership, and Leadership: Validation Is a Power Tool

After Kendall's diagnosis, I let her see me cry. I let her hear me say, "This is hard." I showed her my softness without sacrificing my strength.

She didn't see me as weak. She saw me as *whole*.

That single shift deepened our bond and rewired her own understanding of what courage looks like.

Whether you're a parent, a partner, or a project lead—validation isn't a luxury. It's leadership.

Figure 6.1 – Inner Voice Rewrite ™ Worksheet

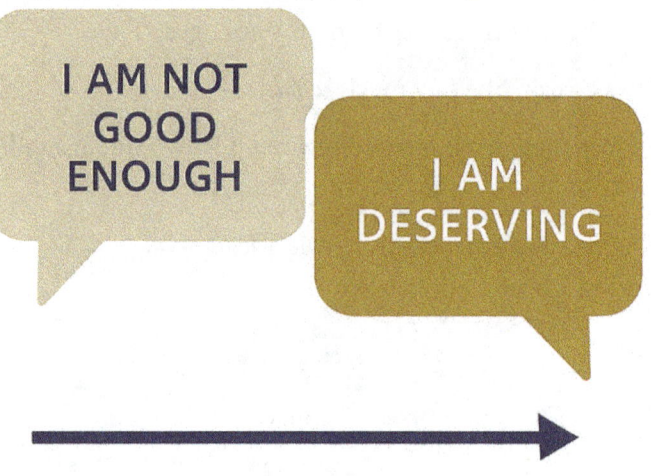

Figure 6.1: The Inner Voice Rewrite™ *helps you confront inherited narratives and rewrite the script in alignment with who you are becoming.*

The *Inner Voice Rewrite*™: A Framework for Emotional Truth

I created a tool I call the *Inner Voice Rewrite*™, a four-step journaling framework that rewires your inner narrative in real-time.

1. Name the Feeling – What emotion is here right now?
2. Locate the Lie – What false belief is this feeling feeding? ("I'm failing." "I'm not enough.")
3. Counter with Compassion – What would you say to your best friend in this moment?
4. Rewrite the Narrative – What truth can you speak over this moment?

Example:

- Feeling: "I'm overwhelmed."
- Lie: "I'm not cut out for this."
- Compassion: "Anyone balancing this much would feel heavy."
- Rewrite: "I'm doing the best I can—and that is worthy."

Real-Life Parallel: Jordan's Redefinition

Jordan, a retired firefighter turned entrepreneur, faced deep imposter syndrome after starting his own consulting firm. He had saved lives in burning buildings—but doubted himself when drafting a proposal.

Through coaching, he uncovered the core belief: "I'm not smart enough for this world."

That belief wasn't rooted in fact. It was rooted in old conditioning. In childhood wounds. In a culture that honored his grit but never affirmed his growth.

Once he validated that emotion and rewrote the story, he showed up differently. Boldly. Bravely. Balanced.

Shift Snapshot: From Wound to Wisdom

Teresa, a former foster youth turned clinical psychologist, built her career on logic and grit. But she avoided her own trauma story for decades.

Finally, she paused.

She journaled. She cried. She visited her former group home. She wrote a letter to her ten-year-old self.

"I had to validate the little girl," she said. "Before I could honor the woman she became."

She now leads trauma-informed trainings nationwide. Her pain? Transformed. Not erased—but redefined.

Your Turn to Shift

Ask yourself:

- What emotion am I minimizing that actually needs acknowledgment?
- What old belief is silently shaping my behavior?
- What would change if I allowed my emotions to *teach* me, not *trap* me?

Then write this affirmation:

"*I honor what I feel. I am not my feelings, but my feelings matter. I am worthy of compassion—even from myself.*"

Say it. Own it. Become it.

Chapter Takeaway

- You can't heal what you refuse to feel. Emotional suppression is not resilience—it's delay.
- Validation isn't weakness. It's emotional intelligence and a gateway to authenticity.

V IS FOR VALIDATE — HONOR IT, DON'T HOST IT

Mirror Moment™

Your space to reflect, reveal, and realign.

Chapter 7

O IS FOR OWN — POWER LOOKS GOOD ON YOU

Unpopular Truth: You can't lead a life you're unwilling to claim.

Ownership begins when you stop waiting for someone else to name your worth. This chapter helps you claim your power—not just the polished parts, but the past, the pivots, and the truth you've tried to downplay. Because power doesn't come from perfection. It comes from possession.

Ownership. It sounds like confidence and echoes like confrontation.

It doesn't arrive with applause. It doesn't wait for consensus. It asks you to stand where you once stumbled. To speak what you once swallowed. To name what was only ever whispered in therapy or prayer.

Ownership isn't about arriving fully formed. It's about showing up—scarred, sacred, and sovereign.

And not just in your wins but in your wounds.
In your truth.
In your becoming.

Setup: The Moment I Took the Mic Back

There was a season when I was everyone's favorite team player. I was exceptional at elevating others—at making their vision shine, their voice heard, their seat secure. But in doing so, I misplaced myself.

From the outside? I was thriving. Multi-million-dollar portfolios. High-stakes operations. Influence. Respect. A seat at tables where women—especially Black women—were rarely invited, much less embraced.

But inside, I felt like a guest in my own story.

Until one day, after leading another major initiative with grace and grit, a colleague leaned in and said, "You're so good at making other people look powerful."

I smiled. But something cracked open.

That sentence haunted me—not because it wasn't a compliment, but because it was the truth I had been avoiding.

I had mastered proximity to power but never claimed my own.

That was the day I stopped being a brand ambassador for someone else's legacy.

That was the day I took the mic back—and started narrating my own.

The Cost of Deferring Your Power

We are conditioned to wait:
Wait for permission.
Wait for praise.
Wait to be chosen.

We're told that confidence is arrogance, that certainty is selfish. Especially if you come from systems that taught you to survive more than thrive.

But here's the quiet cost of deferring your power: you begin to forget your own voice.

Psychologist Julian Rotter (1966) introduced the concept of Locus of Control—the belief that you either shape your life (internal locus) or that life shapes you (external locus).

When we constantly defer decisions, suppress desires, or outsource dreams—we strengthen the lie that power belongs to someone else. And while yes, injustice exists—

yes, gatekeeping is real—owning your life does not mean denying systemic harm. It means refusing to become its permanent tenant.

You can resist a broken system *and* reclaim your own agency.

Ownership is the intersection of grief and grit. It is where you stop rehearsing old scripts and start rewriting the terms.

Narrative Identity, and Role Disruption

According to Dr. Dan McAdams' (2001) narrative identity theory, we form our identity by constructing a life story—a personal myth about who we are, where we come from, and where we're headed.

But too often, our stories aren't authored—they're inherited.

Handed down in the form of roles:
The fixer.
The provider.
The "strong one."
The second-in-command.
The one who never asks for help.

The problem? Those roles may have kept you safe, but they won't make you free.

You can't pivot into a life you don't believe you deserve.

You have to own the pen—even when your hand is shaking.

Real-Life Parallel: From Assigned Role to Authentic Voice

Andre, a brilliant nonprofit administrator, spent years quietly steering million-dollar operations. He was humble. Sharp. Invisible. Others took credit; he took notes.

When his pitch for promotion was denied for the third time—with no feedback, just silence—he quit.

No nest egg. No roadmap. Just a belief: *I can build what I was never given.*

Within a year, Andre launched a consulting firm. He became the strategist behind regional transformation projects. One day, his former execs hired him—at five times his previous salary.

"I thought I needed their endorsement," he told me. "Turns out, I just needed my own."

Ownership doesn't require legacy. It requires *liberation*.

The *Personal Power Audit*™

I created the *Personal Power Audit*™ to help people identify where their power is leaking—and where it's waiting to be reclaimed.

The Audit Questions:

1. Where am I deferring decisions I'm fully capable of making?
2. What role am I playing that no longer fits the life I'm building?
3. What truth am I avoiding because it might disrupt someone else's comfort?
4. Who benefits from me staying small?
5. What does power look and feel like—*for me*?

When you take inventory of your choices, you begin to disrupt inherited scripts. And that's where the real pivot begins.

Figure 8.1 – *Personal Power Audit* ™ **Template**

STRENGTHS	VALUES	BOUNDARIES

Figure 8.1: This Personal Power Audit ™ *helps you locate power leaks in your life and reclaim energy that belongs to your purpose. It's not about force—it's about focus.*

From Narrative Hostage to Narrative Healer

Sasha, a corporate VP, was told—again—that she was "too assertive." She wasn't invited to a strategy summit she'd helped design. The final straw? Being told to "coach her tone."

She resigned the next week.

Now she runs a leadership firm that teaches women—especially women of color—how to turn weaponized feedback into winning strategies.

Sasha didn't just reclaim her power. She multiplied it.

Men, Masculinity, and Silent Shame

Let's also be honest about how patriarchy boxes men out of their own emotional agency.

Omar, a former Marine and small business owner, confessed during a coaching session, "I've always been seen as the rock. But the truth is—I've been cracking for years."

When his son attempted suicide, Omar didn't cry. He got quieter. He handled logistics. He shut down.

His ownership came slowly—through therapy, through journaling, through small acts of softness.

"I realized," he told me, "that being a man didn't mean carrying it all. It meant owning what's mine—and sharing the load."

For both men and women, power expands when we stop *performing* and start *participating* in our own lives.

Resolution: The *P.I.V.O.T.*™ of Ownership

Here's how you use the *P.I.V.O.T.*™ framework to step into your power:

- Pause – Am I reacting from fear or showing up with intention?
- Identify – What belief or narrative is holding me back from owning this moment?
- Validate – What emotion or truth have I been minimizing?
- Own – What action am I responsible for? What authority have I been avoiding?

- Take Action – What decision will affirm the life I say I want?

Power doesn't arrive. It's claimed. Over and over again.

Shift Snapshot: Janelle's Garage Empire

Janelle was laid off after twelve years. Single mom. No plan B. But she had an eye for design—and a garage.

She started hosting pop-up events from that garage. Then corporate retreats. Then weddings. Now? She's a six-figure event strategist featured in *Forbes*.

"The layoff felt like failure," she said. "But it was the door to my own damn kingdom."

Your Turn to Shift

Take a breath. Then ask yourself:

- What version of me have I outgrown?
- Where am I waiting to be rescued when I've already been released?
- What truth am I finally ready to name?

Now say it with your chest:

"I own my past. I own my pace. I own my power. I am not waiting to be chosen—I am choosing myself."

You've reclaimed your voice. You've reentered the room differently. But what happens when the world still says, "Wait?"

You move anyway.

Chapter Takeaway

- Ownership is not perfection—it's personal permission to stop waiting and start leading.
- When you own your story, you stop performing and start transforming.

Mirror Moment™

Your space to reflect, reveal, and realign.

Chapter 8

T IS FOR TAKE ACTION — MOVE WITHOUT PERMISSION

Unpopular Truth: The perfect plan is the enemy of the powerful pivot.

Waiting for the right moment is often the perfect excuse. But movement isn't just a matter of readiness—it's a matter of will. This chapter flips the script on perfectionism and invites you to take action, even if your hands are still shaking.

We wait.
We wait for the stars to align, the email to arrive, the
fear to subside, the nudge to feel divine.

We wait for clarity, for consensus, for certainty. We wait for the room, the budget, the green light. We wait for someone to anoint our dream as worthy.

But what if the green light is not something you wait for?

What if the green light is you?

Setup: When the Plan Didn't Exist, But the Push Did

When I left corrections for aerospace, no one clapped. No one handed me a blueprint. No one said, "Here's your next right step."

I didn't have certainty—I had conviction.

When I launched the Kendall Wyche Foundation, I wasn't "ready." I was raw. But I was also real. And I knew I couldn't keep waiting for permission to move on what I had already been shown in the dark.

That is the power of the T in *P.I.V.O.T.*™—Take Action. Not when you're fully-formed. Not when you're debt-free, doubt-free, or distraction-free.

But now. Even scared. *Especially scared.*

The Tyranny of the "Right Time"

We are seduced by the illusion of perfect timing.

Our culture worships preparation and punishes messiness. We're told to "build the plan" and "wait until it's scalable." We glorify the strategy deck. We romanticize the risk only after someone else has survived it.

But planning without motion is procrastination in Prada.

And here's the kicker: the more brilliant you are, the more likely you are to overthink the leap. Why? Because you can envision every way it could go wrong. You have the receipts, the risk matrix, the report.

You can intellectually dismantle your own destiny.

That's analysis paralysis. It feels like discipline. But it's fear in designer shoes.

Ajzen's Theory of Planned Behavior: Why We Still Don't Move

Social psychologist Icek Ajzen's *Theory of Planned Behavior* (1991) helps explain this paralysis. It tells us that while intention is important, action is driven by one's perceived behavioral control—the belief that you are capable of making a move, regardless of external barriers.

Here's the problem: Most of us confuse uncertainty with inability.

- *"I don't know the next step"* becomes *"I can't take any step."*
- *"I've never done this before"* becomes *"I shouldn't even try."*
- *"I might fail"* becomes *"I'll wait until I can't."*

But movement doesn't require mastery. It requires muscle memory—the kind built through repetition, not perfection.

Pychyl's Theory of Motivation: Motion First, Momentum Follows

Dr. Timothy Pychyl (2013), a behavioral psychologist and procrastination researcher, puts it this way: "We don't wait to feel motivated—we get motivated by doing."

This flips everything we've been told.

Motivation is *not* the spark before the step. It's the result of taking the step.

Action generates emotion. Emotion fuels momentum. And momentum builds confidence.

So the question is not "What inspires me?"

It's "What will I do *before* I feel ready?"

Tool: The *21-Day Micro-Decision Tracker*™

Let me introduce your new companion in motion: the *21-Day Micro-Decision Tracker*™.

It's not a habit tracker. It's not a goal planner. It's a tool for momentum.

Every day, for twenty-one days, you commit to a micro-decision—a single, small action that affirms your vision and builds your capacity.

Sample Entries:

- Day 1: Email someone I admire and introduce myself.
- Day 4: Post one piece of content that aligns with my values.
- Day 5: Call the mentor you've been avoiding—especially if pride was the reason you never followed up.
- Day 7: Write down three people I can serve with my skillset.

- Day 14: Record a video pitching my idea—just for me.
- Day 19: Submit the proposal. Even if it feels "unpolished."

Why it works: Micro-decisions are frictionless. They train your nervous system to associate movement with safety, not danger. And after twenty-one days? You're no longer waiting. You're becoming.

Figure 8.1 – *21-Day Micro-Decision Tracker ™* **Template**

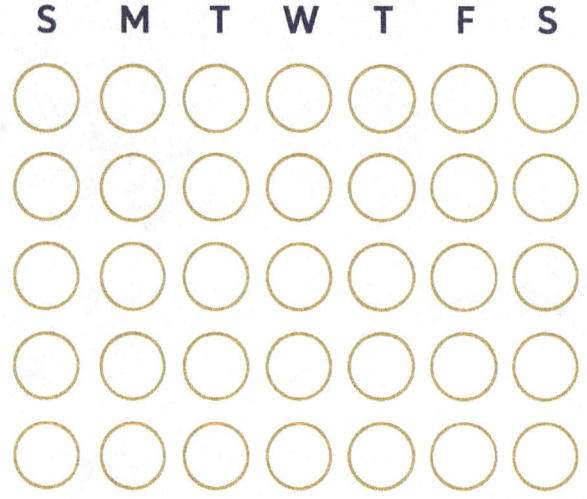

Figure 8.1: Track one decision a day for twenty-one days. The 21-Day Micro-Decision Tracker™ *builds consistency, confidence, and measurable forward motion during any pivot.*

Real-Life Parallel: From Leap to Legacy

Michelle, a senior compliance officer in finance, had a vision to help first-generation students navigate college admissions. But she waited for the "right time" for years. She waited for savings, for support, for certainty.

Then her father passed away unexpectedly. Grief clarified what strategy never could.

She launched a free webinar. Then a mentorship circle. Then a nonprofit.

Today, Michelle's program serves over 3,000 students annually. She told me, "I thought I needed capital. I just needed courage."

Shift Snapshot: From Inmate to Innovator

Niko, wrongfully convicted, served twelve years in prison. When he was released, the doors that were supposed to open for him stayed shut.

So, he built his own.

He learned to code on a public library computer. His first project? A website helping other returning citizens find reentry support. He taught himself. Then taught others.

Today, Niko is a tech entrepreneur employing men who share his past.

Every action he took was imperfect. But every action was a vote for his future.

He didn't ask for permission.

He moved because freedom demanded it.

Cultural Truth: Movement Is Revolutionary

In many cultures—especially marginalized ones—motion has always been a form of rebellion.

Our ancestors didn't wait for policies to shift. They moved through back doors, over bridges, across waters. They made a way using no blueprint. No title. No roadmap. Just faith.

Movement is ancestral.
Movement is sacred.
Movement is your birthright.

Resolution: Move the Energy; Move the Narrative

If you've done the Pause, Identify, Validate, and Own—now it's time to move.

Here's your *P.I.V.O.T.*™ in action:

- Pause: *What's one action that scares me and excites me?*
- Identify: *What's the belief that's trying to keep me safe but small?*
- Validate: *Of course I'm scared. But I trust myself anyway.*
- Own: *This decision belongs to me. This vision has my name on it.*
- Take Action: *Hit send. Start the recording. Make the offer. Take the first brick and build the road beneath your feet.*

Taking action is where your pivot archetype starts to express itself. Whether you're a Strategist pivoting through logic, or a Storyweaver shifting through meaning, action reveals identity. The more I studied this, the more I realized *High PQ*™ isn't just a framework—it's an ecosystem.

Your Turn to Shift

Ask yourself:

- What's the smallest possible move I can make today that honors my next chapter?
- What have I postponed because I feared looking messy?
- Whose approval am I still waiting for—and why?

Now declare this aloud:

"I move, not because I am certain, but because I am called. I don't need a guarantee to begin. I am the green light."

Action creates shift. But how do you measure the strength of your comeback?

Enter: The *Pivot Quotient*™.

Chapter Takeaway

- Action is the antidote to doubt. You don't wait for confidence—you build it through movement.
- Small decisions stack. Movement, even messy, is momentum.

T IS FOR TAKE ACTION — MOVE WITHOUT PERMISSION

Mirror Moment™

Your space to reflect, reveal, and realign.

Case Study
Zoom – A Masterclass in High PQ™

Case Overview:

When COVID-19 shut down the world, Zoom became the backbone of human connection. While competitors scrambled, Zoom didn't just react; it pivoted with precision. By pausing strategically, identifying market shifts, validating solutions, owning its shortcomings, and taking bold action, Zoom showcased what high *Pivot Quotient*™ (PQ) looks like in motion.

P.I.V.O.T. **™ Overlay:**

- **Pause:** Before responding to the surge, Zoom paused to analyze infrastructure demands. This allowed for scaling cloud capacity to handle a 30x spike in usage.
- **Identify:** Zoom spotted the migration of work, school, and social connection to virtual platforms. Their shift from an enterprise-only strategy to an inclusive "video for everyone" approach captured new markets.
- **Validate:** They launched free education accounts, used rapid feedback loops, and iterated in real-time (adding breakout rooms, security features, and virtual backgrounds).
- **Own:** When "Zoom-bombing" security concerns emerged, the company addressed them head-on. CEO Eric Yuan publicly owned the problem and launched a ninety-day security overhaul.
- **Take Action:** Zoom democratized access globally, creating flexible pricing and new features for both organizations and individuals.

PQ Score (Zoom):

Pause – 5 | Identify – 5 | Validate – 5 | Own – 4 | Take Action – 5 → **24/25 (*high PQ*)**

Reflection Prompt:

"What would it look like for you or your team to adopt Zoom-level speed and strategic clarity in your next pivot?"

> **Pro Tip:** The proof is in the pivot. For a deeper look at how transformation scales in business and beyond, check out *The Spiral Effect: Case Studies in Pivot, Proof, and Possibility.*

PART III

THE RISE – Pivoting as a Way of Life

Chapter 8.5

INTRODUCING *PIVOT QUOTIENT*™: THE MISSING ELEMENT

Unpopular Truth: Most people will never master it—because it requires confronting the parts of themselves they've spent a lifetime avoiding.

Chapter 9

THE BOUNCE QUOTIENT: WHY SPEED OUTWEIGHS SPECTACLE

Unpopular Truth: The world gives applause for rising eventually—but legacy belongs to those who rise strategically.

What if resilience wasn't just about bouncing back—but about how you recalibrate forward? This chapter unpacks The Pivot Quotient™ *(PQ), a game-changing metric that redefines success not by what you avoid, but by how quickly you recover, realign, and respond.*

This is the metric no one tracks but everyone should.

We obsess over how far people rise. How fast they ascend. How loud their victories echo. But what if the real secret to sustainable success isn't in the *height* of the jump—but in the *speed* of the return?

Let me ask you something personal:

How quickly do you come back to yourself after you've been knocked flat?

How long does it take you to lace up your purpose, re-tie your boundaries, and return—not just to the work, but to your worth?

Resilience isn't a spectacle. It's not glitzy. It rarely goes viral. But it's the one trait that separates those who make a comeback from those who make excuses.

I've come to learn that bounce-back speed is a truer reflection of leadership than any performance review.

Because life doesn't reward the tallest leaps.

Life rewards the *quickest pivots*.

Knocked Down, Not Knocked Out

I didn't always measure life in bounce-back speed. For years, I measured success by degrees, promotions, applause.

Until the fall came. And silence followed.

I had just landed a leadership role in elder care—an industry that touched me deeply after caregiving for my grandmother.

I was on fire with purpose. Until the pay didn't match the promise. Until the progress I was sold came wrapped in politics. Until the leader who looked like me kept her mouth shut while I got squeezed.

That moment didn't break me. But it broke my *tolerance*.

So, I walked. No job. No fallback plan. Just a raw conviction that peace was more profitable than a paycheck poisoned by compromise.

That fall? It became a turning point. Because I didn't stay down. I got back up—*faster*.

The Metric That Really Matters

That moment was my resilience gym. And I've lifted heavier since.

Dr. Angela Duckworth (2007) calls it grit—passion and perseverance for long-term goals. Dr. Carol Dweck (2006) calls it a growth mindset—the belief that abilities develop through effort.

But in elite performance psychology, we use another term:

Recovery Time Objective (RTO)

RTO originated in IT and disaster planning. It asks:

How long can a system be down before it must be restored to full function?

Now apply that to your life:

- How long can you be down before you rise again?
- How long before your pivot kicks in?

Your emotional RTO might be the most important metric you're not tracking.

Because the quicker you recover, the more resilient you become. The more resilient you become, the faster you flourish.

When I left corrections for aerospace, I wasn't "qualified." But my bounce-back speed? Unmatched.

I knew how to perform under pressure, learn in motion, and pivot with precision.

Introducing the *Pivot Quotient*™

Just like IQ measures intelligence and EQ measures emotional intelligence, your *Pivot Quotient*™ (PQ) measures your capacity to recover from failure and return to forward momentum.

PQ = Your ability to Process Internalized Vulnerability into Optimal Transformation.

High PQ™ individuals aren't defined by how much they endure—but by how quickly they respond, reframe, and re-engage with purpose.

Pivot Quotient™ **Reflects:**

- Recovery time after setbacks (emotional RTO)
- Ability to extract lessons from failure
- Willingness to move without full certainty
- Consistent self-leadership under pressure

This book is your *Pivot Quotient*™ builder.

We will track, train, and transform how you rise.

Figure 9.1 – *Pivot Quotient™* Self-Assessment Visual

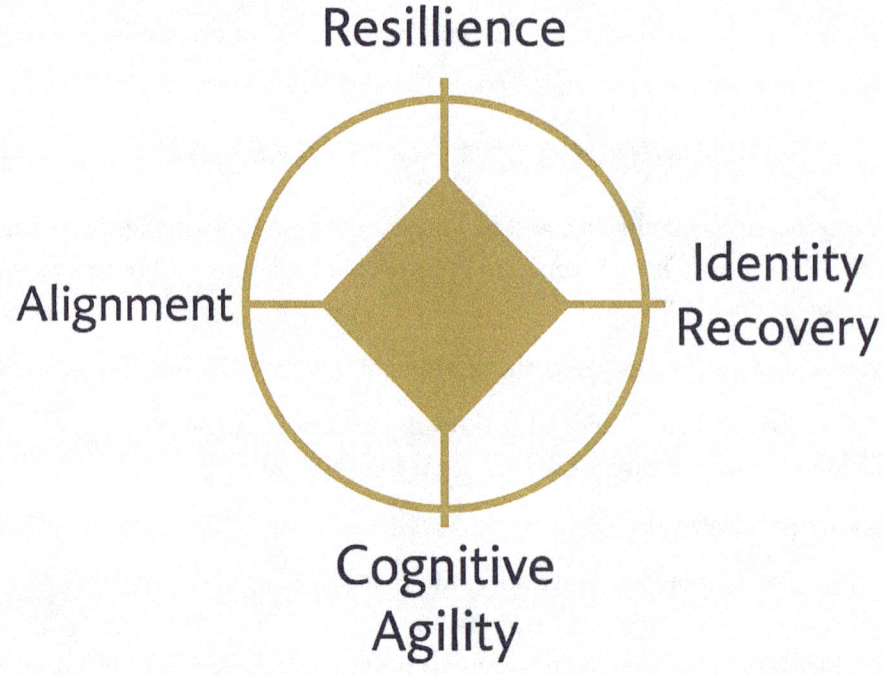

Figure 9.1: The Pivot Quotient™ *is your personalized resilience profile. This visual captures the four dimensions of* High PQ™ *and reflects how aligned your pivot capacity currently is.*

Resolution: Fail Fast, Recover Faster

Great leaders don't avoid failure. They embrace it. But what sets them apart is how fast they recover.

Let's name a few:

- Simone Biles, who paused her career to preserve her mind—and returned stronger.
- Sara Blakely, who stacked rejections into a billion-dollar business.
- Barack Obama, who turned obstacles into oratory and opposition into opportunity.

They didn't let the fall define them. They used it to refine them.

Don't waste years recovering from one rejection. Take fifteen minutes. Then choose your next move.

The Bounce Refrain

You fell. But you're not finished. You cried. But you're not crushed. You stumbled. But you're still sacred.

You're still standing. You're still becoming.

And the faster you believe that, the faster you bounce.

Application: Track the Right Metrics

We've tracked the wrong things for too long:

- Likes instead of lessons.
- Claps instead of clarity.
- Heights instead of healing.

Here's what to track now:

1. Emotional RTO: How long does it take me to move from pain to plan?
2. Pivot Point: What is my signal to shift?
3. Recovery Ritual: What routines restore me fastest?
4. *Pivot Quotient*™ (PQ): How consistently do I convert adversity into agency?

Try this:

- Keep a *Bounce-Back Journal*™
- After every setback, write:
  - What happened?
  - How did I respond?
  - What will I do differently?
  - How fast did I move from stuck to strategic?

Time it. Celebrate the bounce—not just the win.

Shift Snapshot: From Crash to Clarity

Deja, a brilliant data analyst, was laid off with forty-eight hours' notice. She spiraled. Questioned her worth. Replayed every meeting where she dimmed her light.

But on Day 3, she got up. On Day 4, she updated her resume. By Day 7, she had a job interview.

By Week 2, she had an offer.

"I stopped looking for a silver lining," she told me. "I became the lining."

Your Turn to Shift

Ask yourself:

- What's one fall I've never fully rebounded from?
- What belief about failure am I still rehearsing?
- What would it look like to bounce—not bitterly, but better?

Now say it: "I bounce back like it's my birthright."

Because it is.

And because bounce-back speed isn't just a concept—it's a capability—I created the *PQ Inventory*™ to help you locate yourself on the resilience spectrum. This isn't your average self-assessment; this is a mirror and a map. It probes deeper than personality tests or performance reviews, asking not just how you behave—but how you rebuild. It evaluates four core dimensions: *Emotional Regulation Under Pressure* (ERUPT), *Speed of Cognitive Reframing* (SCR), *Identity Differentiation Index* (IDI), and *Purposeful Adaptation Capacity* (PAC). In other words, how fast do you bounce? How well do you reframe? How clearly do you know yourself beyond your roles? And how courageously do you adapt with purpose, not panic?

Rooted in Bandura's self-efficacy theory and fortified by trauma-informed leadership models, the *PQ Inventory*™ invites you to measure what has long gone unmeasured: the precision of your pivots. Because true resilience is not a return to who you were—it's a recalibration into who you were becoming all along. This tool gives language to your internal shift patterns. It dignifies the silent recoveries, the quick recalibrations, the invisible strength it takes to lead after loss or rebuild after rupture. You won't just find numbers here. You'll find narrative. You'll find nuance. You'll find *you*. And that, in this moment, is the most powerful data point of all.

Figure 9.2 – *PQ Inventory*™ Assessment Page.

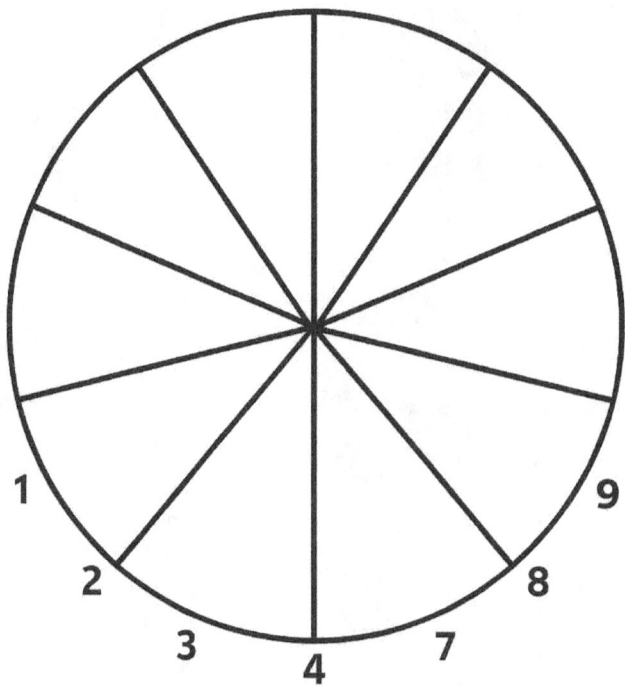

Figure 9.2: The PQ Inventory™ *helps you assess your readiness and resilience across identity, agility, emotional regulation, and alignment.*

Beyond the Bounce: What Type of Pivot Are You In?

Not every pivot comes from collapse. Not every shift begins in crisis. And not every evolution requires breaking down to break through.

In the *High PQ™* model, we honor the **full spectrum of pivot triggers**. Whether your pivot is emerging from exhaustion or rising from vision, each one demands its own kind of power—and all of them build your *Pivot Quotient™*.

The Three Types of Pivots:

1. Disruptive Pivots

Born from breakdown, burnout, injustice, trauma, or grief. These are the pivots no one asks for but many of us are forced to navigate. They often begin with rupture and lead to revelation.

2. Discernment Pivots

Born from quiet knowing, legacy alignment, or the realization that your current chapter no longer fits. These pivots are chosen—intentionally, unapologetically. They're rooted in clarity, not crisis.

3. Divine Pivots

Born from ancestral pull, spiritual instruction, or sacred timing. Divine pivots may not be logical—but they are *aligned*. These are the pivots led by faith, not fear.

Your pivot may not look like someone else's. It doesn't have to. What matters is that it's real, it's yours, and it's done with intention.

We've glamorized the dramatic comeback. The headline-worthy leap. The big bounce. But what if the boldest flex isn't the bounce height—it's your recovery velocity?

What if you could *track* that comeback muscle? What if resilience wasn't just a feeling—but a measurable, trainable force?

Chapter Takeaway

- The true measure of resilience isn't how high you leap—it's how quickly you realign after the fall.
- Your ability to respond, recalibrate, and restart is your real superpower.

Mirror Moment™

Your space to reflect, reveal, and realign.

Chapter 9.5

THE PIVOT QUOTIENT™: RESILIENCE REIMAGINED

Unpopular Truth: It's not how high you leap, but how fast you learn to land.

Recovery isn't about erasing difficulty—it's about embodying your ability to adapt and rise. In this chapter, we elevate PQ into a core leadership and life skill, defending it not just as a framework but as a legacy principle that changes how we navigate every storm.

When the Bounce Became the Battle

It was 3:27 a.m. I was sitting on the cold tile of the hospital bathroom floor, my back pressed against the door, my head in my hands. Kendall's glucose levels had crashed again. Alarms beeped. Nurses rushed. I had done everything right, and yet, here we were—again.

I wanted to crumble. But crumbling wasn't an option.

So, I rose. Not because I felt strong. But because I'd trained my spirit to rebound faster than my fear.

That moment wasn't cinematic. It was cellular. My nervous system had been rewired by years of navigating high-stakes environments—from corrections to corporate, from motherhood to movement-building. My bounce-back speed had become my survival strategy.

And that's when I realized: intelligence (IQ) and emotional insight (EQ) were not enough. What mattered most—what saved me—was my PQ: *Pivot Quotient*™.

What Is PQ?

If IQ is how we think, and EQ is how we feel, PQ is how we recalibrate.

Your *Pivot Quotient*™ (PQ) is your internal measure of recovery, adaptability, and embodied resilience in the face of disruption.

It answers the question:

"How quickly can you return to clarity, courage, and conscious action after chaos?"

Think of it as your spiritual and strategic elasticity. Not whether you fall—but how you land. Not how long you stayed down—but how intentionally you got back up.

Bounce height is what the world claps for. Bounce speed is what legacy requires.

The Theory Behind PQ: *P.I.V.O.T* ™ in Action

PQ isn't just about willpower. It's a learned, repeatable response rooted in both science and soul.

Let's break down PQ through the *P.I.V.O.T.*™ framework:

- **P** – Pause: PQ starts with nervous system regulation. The ability to *pause* interrupts panic and creates space for discernment. This echoes polyvagal theory, which emphasizes the need for a calm state to access executive function (Porges, 2011).
- **I** – Identify: *High PQ*™ individuals don't deny disruption—they name it. Identifying the *root* of a reaction builds metacognition and strengthens one's internal locus of control (Rotter, 1966).
- **V** – Validate: PQ is emotional agility in action (David, 2016). It's not bypassing feelings—it's recognizing that emotions are information, not instruction.

- **O – Own:** Ownership is where your narrative shifts. *High PQ™* means reclaiming your agency—not by pretending the fall didn't happen, but by claiming how you'll rise from it. It aligns with narrative identity theory (McAdams, 2001).
- **T – Take Action:** The final mile. PQ requires not just introspection but integration. Small moves that compound into sustainable recovery. Think Pychyl's motivation loop—action begets motivation (Pychyl, 2013).

Addressing the Critics: The Unapologetic Defense

Let's name the doubt before it enters the room.

Critique 1: Isn't this just another resilience buzzword?

No. Resilience is often spoken of as an abstract trait—innate or acquired. PQ is a measurable, actionable *response strategy*. It's not how much you've suffered; it's how swiftly you re-engage your power after suffering.

Critique 2: Doesn't bounce-back culture risk glamorizing overperformance and burnout?

PQ isn't about rushing recovery. It's about *authentic recovery*. The pause is part of the speed. Stillness is baked into the reactivation. Bounce-back does not mean bypass. It means recalibrate *honestly*, then re-engage *intentionally*.

Critique 3: Is PQ only for high achievers?

No. PQ is for anyone living through uncertainty. For fathers trying to hold it together after job loss. For single mothers crying in their cars between meetings. For students redefining themselves after rejection. PQ is universal. It's human.

Tools: Measure and Strengthen Your PQ

1. PQ Tracker™ (21-Day Edition)

Inspired by habit formation science, this micro-movement tracker invites you to record:

- Disruption Event (what threw you off)
- Reaction Time (how long before you re-centered)
- Response Strategy Used (pause, reframe, journal, ask for help, etc.)
- Bounce-Back Quality (from 1–10: clarity, peace, forward motion)

Over twenty-one days, you'll start to see patterns. You'll learn what accelerates your bounce—and what blocks it.

2. Journal Prompts

- When was the last time I surprised myself with how I recovered?
- What emotional detours do I tend to take before returning to alignment?
- What would my highest self say to me in my lowest moment?
- What's one disruption I thought would destroy me… but didn't?

Real-Life Examples of *High PQ™* Pivots

Carlos is a firefighter who returned to duty after losing his brother to the same blaze that nearly took his own life. His PQ wasn't in forgetting the grief. It was in using it to become a mental health advocate for first responders.

Mei is a small business owner whose bakery burned down during protests. She journaled daily, launched pop-ups with donated ingredients, and turned her resilience story into a viral TEDx talk.

Tariq is a college student from a refugee family who failed out of his first semester. He joined a student support group, reframed his sense of identity, and now runs a mentorship program for at-risk students.

PQ isn't about who bounces highest. It's about who learns to land—again and again.

Final Word: Recovery Is a Rebellion

Let me be clear: this is not a call to perform resilience for the comfort of others. This is a call to practice resilience for the liberation of self.

PQ isn't about perfection. It's about *permission*—to heal, to pivot, to rise.

You've survived. Now it's time to measure your capacity to return—not to who you were, but to who you're becoming.

And the speed of that return?
That's your *Pivot Quotient*™.

Call to Action:

Say it out loud:

"I don't just bounce back. I bounce forward. With clarity. With courage. With speed that honors my soul."

Track it. Trust it. Teach it.

Let your bounce become your blueprint.

Because it's not how high you leap. It's how fast you learn to land.

And baby, you've got air.

Chapter Takeaways

- PQ is not about how high you climb—it's about how quickly you recover, recalibrate, and return.
- PQ turns resilience from a buzzword into a measurable, embodied practice.

Mirror Moment™

Your space to reflect, reveal, and realign.

Case Study
J.Crew – A Failure to Pivot

Case Overview:

Once a dominant force in retail, J.Crew filed for bankruptcy in 2020. While external factors such as debt and shifting consumer habits played a role, the deeper issue was a failure to pivot. The company's inability to pause, identify, validate, own, and take action decisively serves as a cautionary tale for leaders who underestimate disruption.

P.I.V.O.T.™ Overlay:

- **Pause:** J.Crew never paused to assess its mounting debt or declining mall traffic, focusing instead on short-term sales fixes.
- **Identify:** It failed to recognize the accelerating dominance of e-commerce and consumer demand for digital-first shopping experiences.
- **Validate:** There was no meaningful testing of subscription models, partnerships, or hybrid retail innovations that might have reversed its decline.
- **Own:** Leadership delayed acknowledging the debt crisis, opting for incremental strategies rather than transformative decisions.
- **Take Action:** By the time J.Crew acted, competitors like Zara and ASOS had already captured the digital-native market.

PQ Score (J.Crew):

Pause – 2 | Identify – 2 | Validate – 1 | Own – 2 | Take Action – 2 → **9/25 (low PQ)**

Reflection Prompt:

"Where in your organization do you see J.Crew-level inertia? Which P.I.V.O.T.™ step could break that cycle first?"

For a full analysis with supporting data, see Appendix C: The J.Crew Case Study.

> **Pro Tip:** The proof is in the pivot. For a deeper look at how transformation scales in business and beyond, check out *The Spiral Effect: Case Studies in Pivot, Proof, and Possibility.*

Chapter 10
SHIFT CULTURE, NOT JUST CIRCUMSTANCES

Unpopular truth: You cannot out-journal systemic oppression. You cannot meditate away misogyny. You cannot breathe your way out of a boardroom built without you in mind.

Personal growth is powerful, but cultural transformation is essential. This chapter disrupts the myth that mindset alone can free us and challenges us to pivot in ways that shift systems—not just situations. Because change without structural awareness is just survival on repeat.

We've been sold a half-truth wrapped in glittery ambition: that personal growth is the key to liberation. That if you optimize your morning routine, manifest the dream job, read enough leadership books, and lean in with just the right posture—you'll break through.

But here's the whole truth:
Mindset without system change is martyrdom in disguise.
You are not broken. The system is rigged.

The Rise of Systems-Aware Self-Leadership

Let's name what this really is: structural fatigue.

You are tired, not because you're weak, but because you're swimming against currents designed to drown you in microaggressions, gendered expectations, inaccessible policies, and inherited silence. The bootstraps fable never factored in intersectionality.

Dr. Kimberlé Crenshaw's (1989) intersectionality theory teaches us that oppression isn't a single-axis experience. It's layered, like grief, like code-switching, like generational trauma passed off as "tradition." Women of color, neurodivergent folks, queer leaders, working-class visionaries—we aren't just navigating glass ceilings. We're climbing *invisible walls with barbed wire.*

Enter: Systems-aware Self-leadership.

This isn't just a new buzzword. It's a revolution. It's what happens when you stop blaming your imposter syndrome and start interrogating your environment. It's when your healing includes policy analysis. When your pivot includes advocacy. And when your legacy includes collective liberation.

The Architecture Was Never Neutral

Let's be honest. The workplace wasn't designed for most of us—it was inherited from industrial systems built by and for a privileged few.

When I first became a healthcare administrator inside a corrections facility, I walked in with my resume in one hand and my righteousness in the other. I believed systems rewarded integrity. I believed doing good was enough. But quickly, I realized: systems don't reward excellence—they protect tradition.

And tradition has a preference.
It has a color.
It has a gender.
It has a pedigree.

It wasn't just policies I was navigating. It was codes. Side-eyes. Assumptions that shrunk me before I ever spoke.

I wasn't crazy. I was coded out of belonging.

Sociologist Patricia Hill Collins (1990) named it *"the matrix of domination"*—the web where racism, sexism, classism, and ableism intersect to form a trap, then gaslight you for feeling caught in it. But naming it? That's where the pivot begins.

The Myth of Empowerment

You can't empowerment-coach your way through a system that profits from your silence.

Empowerment culture—when not paired with equity strategy—becomes a shiny form of shame.

- "You just need a better mindset."
- "Be more confident."
- "Ask for the raise."

But what happens when HR policies gatekeep transparency? What happens when you're labeled aggressive for advocating? What happens when your leadership is brilliant but not "polished" enough for the panel?

You end up like too many of us: leading in whispers. Softening feedback. Dimming brilliance. Silencing instincts.

That's not empowerment. That's survival.

As Rosabeth Moss Kanter (1979) taught us, "Power is the ability to get things done despite resistance." But many of us are so busy resisting invisibility that we have no time left to build impact.

Policy Pivots, and Profiles in Power

Let's talk about what it means to pivot the system.

Alicia, a Black Latina civil engineer in a coastal city, kept watching her neighborhood flood with no intervention. Instead of another letter to the editor, she ran for city council. Her platform: climate justice *and* community inclusion. She won. She now allocates FEMA funding through an equity lens.

Jermaine, a formerly incarcerated father, couldn't find housing. So, he lobbied. He partnered with local nonprofits and pushed for "Ban the Box" legislation in housing. It passed. His pivot wasn't professional—it was policy-driven.

Mira, a tech executive, noticed that her company celebrated Diversity Month but hired from the same three schools. She initiated a scholarship and internship pipeline from community colleges and HBCUs. She didn't just shift the culture—she seeded it.

These aren't rebels. They're architects.
They're not fixing broken things.
They're *building new blueprints.*

The Resistance is Real—But So Is Your Power

This work is exhausting. No sugarcoating that.

When you constantly speak up, you're labeled angry.
When you don't, you're called complicit.
When you pivot loudly, you're disruptive.
When you pivot quietly, you're invisible.

This is structural fatigue—a term coined to describe the mental, emotional, and physiological exhaustion from navigating inequitable systems while trying to transform them.

The solution isn't just rest—it's reimagination.

It's the decision to shift from "what role do I play in this culture?" to "what culture do I want to create from this role?"

The Pivot Is Political

Yes, personal pivots can be powerful. But the most potent pivots are *political*—not in partisanship, but in practice.

A pivot becomes political when it:

- Questions the structure that made the burnout inevitable.
- Refuses silence where inequity screams.
- Puts legacy above likability.

The *P.I.V.O.T.*™ framework lives here, too:

- Pause – Long enough to recognize the system.
- Identify – Where you're absorbing blame that belongs to bias.
- Validate – That your frustration is not overreaction—it's resistance.
- Own – Your right to redesign the space, not just survive in it.

- Take Action – Not just personally. Systemically. Strategically. Sustainably.

Tactical Tools: Your *System-Shift Starter Kit*™

Use these to move from frustration to formation:

1. Bias Audit

Ask:

- What behaviors are rewarded here?
- Whose voices dominate meetings?
- Who gets grace? Who gets correction?

2. Cultural Credo

Write your own three-point leadership manifesto. Mine includes:

- Compassion is not a weakness.
- Transparency is a leadership skill.
- Equity is not nice-to-have. It's non-negotiable.

3. Liberation Metrics

Instead of chasing generic KPIs (Key Performance Indicators), define your LPIs—Legacy Performance Indicators:

- How many voices did I amplify this quarter?
- What system did I challenge, even gently?
- Did I rest in a way that resists capitalism's grip?

Final Word: Shift the Container, Not Just the Contents

You can change jobs and still feel unsafe.
You can gain power and still feel invisible.
You can earn awards and still walk on eggshells.
Why? Because culture is the container. And if it's cracked, your pivot leaks.

Let this be your new rule:

Don't just shift your title. Shift the table. Shift the terms. Shift the timeline.

You don't just belong in the room. You belong in the *rebuild* of the room. You are not just a leader. You are a *liberator*. A blueprint-breaker. A system-shifter.

Patterns don't change through force—they change through frameworks. That's why I began mapping not just individual pivots, but collective ones. The Pivot Ecosystem emerged: a loop that starts with internal disruption and ripples outward—reshaping relationships, teams, and systems.

Shifting systems requires belief that the future can look different. That belief? It's born in science—and in the soul.

Chapter Takeaway

- You can't mindset your way out of systems designed to suppress you.
- Culture is the container. If you want lasting change, shift the space—not just your shoes.

HIGH PQ™

Mirror Moment™

Your space to reflect, reveal, and realign.

Case Study
Department of Corrections – A Systemic PQ Deficit

Case Overview:

The COVID-19 pandemic exposed deep cracks in correctional systems across the U.S. Overcrowding, staff shortages, and operational rigidity compounded the crisis. Without a pivot-ready framework, the Department of Corrections (DOC) was left reactive rather than adaptive, leading to escalating safety concerns, workforce burnout, and public scrutiny.

P.I.V.O.T.™ Overlay:

- **Pause:** There was no systemic pause to assess operational vulnerabilities or create a coordinated response plan.
- **Identify:** DOC failed to recognize early warning signs of staff attrition and inmate unrest due to prolonged lockdowns.
- **Validate:** Unlike other sectors that borrowed best practices from healthcare or crisis management, DOC remained siloed, missing opportunities for collaborative solutions.
- **Own:** Resistance to cultural reform limited transparency and slowed policy changes.
- **Take Action:** Instead of implementing agile staffing models or mental health programs, DOC defaulted to outdated protocols.

PQ Score (DOC):

Pause – 1 | Identify – 2 | Validate – 1 | Own – 2 | Take Action – 1 → **7/25 (critical PQ deficit)**

Reflection Prompt:

"Where do you see DOC-level operational blind spots in your organization? How would applying 'ownership' change the outcome?"

> **Pro Tip:** The proof is in the pivot. For a deeper look at how transformation scales in business and beyond, check out *The Spiral Effect: Case Studies in Pivot, Proof, and Possibility.*

Chapter 11
THE LEGACY PIVOT

Unpopular Truth: Not everyone you love will clap when you break the curse they survived.

Legacy is not what you leave behind—it's what you build in real time. This chapter unpacks how purpose, planning, and pivots intersect to create impact that outlives us. It's time to shape a future that reflects your values, not just your victories.

We love the idea of legacy—until it dares to interrupt tradition. Until it stretches us beyond the blueprint of survival and into the burden of being first. First to name what isn't working. First to heal what is hidden. First to rise and risk being misunderstood by those we love the most.

Legacy doesn't start with applause. It starts with audacity.

PIVOT Isn't Personal—It's Generational

We're often told that pivots are personal: a reinvention, a career switch, a fresh start. But the truth is bolder: your pivot isn't just yours—it's your bloodline's turning point.

Every time you choose healing over hiding, truth over tradition, alignment over approval—you move the entire narrative forward. You don't just break cycles. You rewrite scripts. You disrupt inheritance. You heal family trees by repairing your own root system.

When you pivot, you don't just change your life.
You redirect the future.
You rewire the past.
You reveal what's possible.

That's legacy.

Inheriting What Was Never Healed

Legacy pivots don't begin with big bank accounts or marble plaques. They begin in quiet resistance. In decisions to stop carrying what never belonged to you.

I didn't just inherit my mother's laugh or her love. I inherited her labor. Her loneliness. Her limits. And for years, I mistook those scars for standards.

Like so many daughters, I honored her struggle by reenacting it. Until I realized: the best way to honor the women before me was not to mirror them, but to heal what mirrored through me.

"I want better for my child" is a prayer.
Living that better is the answer.

Building While Bleeding: The Weight of Being First

There's no manual for being the first in your family to say no.

No syllabus for choosing therapy over silence.
No map for creating something that's never existed.
No applause for boundaries that look like betrayal.

As Dr. Murray Bowen (1978) outlined in his family systems theory, the concept of "differentiation" isn't about disconnection—it's about clarity. You are allowed to evolve without apology. You are allowed to love them and still leave their expectations behind.

Being the "first" is heavy—but it's holy.

It's building with borrowed bricks and God's blueprints.
It's failing forward in the dark and daring to call that movement.
It's messy. It's sacred. It's enough.

Resolution: Institutions Over Income

Money is part of legacy—but not all of it. Legacy without infrastructure is a wish. Legacy with strategy is a movement.

That's why I created the Kendall Wyche Foundation—not for credit, but for continuation. Because my daughter's diagnosis demanded a pivot from pain to policy. It required more than a meal plan—it needed a mission.

And that's why the Civilian Corrections Academy exists. Because transformation inside broken systems starts with education, not just empathy.

Your pivot isn't just what you *survive*. It's what you *institutionalize*.

Don't just create income.
Create infrastructure.
Don't just build wealth.
Build wells that others can drink from.

What You Refuse, You Reframe

You are not obligated to pass down your pain.

You can say no. You can say, "Not anymore." You can love the people who raised you while refusing the rules that confined them.

Here's what they won't tell you about legacy:

- It often looks like disobedience to those still surviving.
- It feels like loneliness before it feels like liberation.
- It requires boundaries that echo louder than blessings.

But here's what I *will* tell you: your pivot is permission for someone else to breathe deeper.

Application: Make Legacy Tangible

Legacy can't just be conceptual. It has to be concrete. Here's how to make it real:

- Legacy Journal: Keep a record of every generational decision. Every "first." Every refusal. These are not just moments—they're blueprints.

- Teach While You Build: Invite the next generation to shadow you. Let them see you work, wobble, and win. Normalize visibility.
- Establish Family Practices: Sunday finance check-ins. Gratitude circles. Monthly "what I learned" meetings. Rituals matter.
- Create What Doesn't Exist: A scholarship. A fund. A business. A family document of shared values. Give form to the formless.
- Honor the Ancestors By Becoming the Answer: Make healing the tradition they never had.

Shift Snapshot: My Daughter, My Mirror

When Kendall was diagnosed, I wasn't just grieving her condition—I was confronting a generational ghost. The silence that creeps into rooms where health is a mystery, and resources are scarce. The shame that keeps us quiet when we should be asking questions. The exhaustion of carrying legacy with no roadmap.

But we pivoted.

And every needle, every late-night reading, every hard conversation—that was legacy, too. Not the legacy of pain, but the legacy of presence. Of action. Of advocacy.

We didn't just survive her diagnosis.
We repurposed it.
And that? That is the legacy I'm proud of.

Final Prompt: What Will You Be Remembered For?

You won't be remembered for playing small to stay safe.
You'll be remembered for the sacred risk to shift.
To pivot.
To build while bleeding.
To rise without a manual.
To break what needed breaking—so something better could begin.

Legacy isn't a logo.
It's the look in your child's eyes when they believe they can.
It's the breath of a family no longer bound by silence.
It's the system you rewrote. The truth you lived.
The grace you gave yourself to evolve.

So, if you've been waiting for permission to lead a legacy pivot, this is it.
If not you, then who?
If not now, then when?

Say yes.
Shift anyway.
Let them call it rebellion.
You'll know it was restoration.

Chapter Takeaways

- Resilience isn't theoretical—it shows up in leadership, legacy, and everyday decisions.
- Real-world pivot stories remind us that reinvention is universal and transferable across industries.

THE LEGACY PIVOT

Mirror Moment™

Your space to reflect, reveal, and realign.

PART IV

The Infrastructure of *High PQ*™

Chapter 12

THE SCIENCE OF THE PIVOT

Unpopular Truth: Transformation isn't just a mindset—it's a biological rebellion.

Every transformation looks like chaos in the middle. But beneath the fog of disruption lies a biological blueprint. You are not just reacting to change—you are wired for it. Neuroplasticity tells us that your brain is capable of rerouting, rewiring, and reimagining itself with every challenge you face. That's not just science—it's spiritual architecture. In this chapter, we'll bridge research with lived experience to show how every pivot you make is not a breakdown, but a biochemical breakthrough.

We talk about change like it's an attitude. Like it's something you decide one day, manifest into a Pinterest board, and repeat until you believe it.

But real transformation—lasting, embodied, identity-altering transformation—isn't that neat.

It's not a mantra. It's a molecular event.

It's your brain rewiring. Your body unlearning. Your nervous system breaking up with its addiction to survival.

This chapter is for the pivoters who want to understand what's happening under the hood. Because it's not just that you're changing—it's that your biology is catching up to your bravery.

Neuroplasticity: The Brain's Love Affair With Change

Neuroplasticity is the brain's ability to rewire itself based on new experiences, environments, and behaviors. Once believed to be fixed by adulthood, we now know the brain remains adaptive well into our later years (Doidge, 2007). That means your pivot isn't just personal—it's neurological.

When you disrupt your normal routine—leave the job, break the cycle, rewrite the story—you're not just shifting mindset. You're reprogramming neural pathways conditioned by decades of repetition.

That anxiety you feel when you take a new path? That's your amygdala firing warnings based on old scripts. But when you persist—when you move despite fear—you strengthen your prefrontal cortex, the region responsible for decision-making and future planning.

Your courage has a neural signature.

Identity Disruption: Who Am I Without the Wound?

Let's get honest: one of the scariest parts of the pivot is identity loss.

You don't just leave a job. You leave a title. A story. A sense of self.

You don't just heal the trauma. You bury the version of you that learned how to survive it.

Dr. Bruce Perry (2006) explains that trauma can encode identity through hypervigilance, people-pleasing, overachievement, or emotional numbing. When you begin healing, you don't just lose pain—you lose a coping identity.

And identity disruption is disorienting.

But here's the invitation: what if the grief you feel isn't failure, but freedom loosening its grip on your former self?

You're not breaking down. You're breaking form.

Embodied Change: The Body Keeps the Breakthrough

You can't pivot with your brain alone. Because trauma is stored somatically—in the tissues, not just the thoughts (van der Kolk, 2014). Your body remembers what your mind rationalizes away.

That's why talk therapy alone doesn't always create full integration.

You need practices that involve the body:

- Breathwork to regulate your nervous system.
- Movement (dance, walking, yoga) to express and release stored tension.
- Somatic journaling: Where in your body do you feel the resistance to this next step?

Embodied pivots don't just look like bold decisions. They sound like exhaling shame. They feel like walking differently. Sleeping more peacefully. Crying without panic.

That's healing with hips and heart.

The SCARF Model + Trauma-Informed Transition

Dr. David Rock's SCARF model identifies five social domains that influence human behavior in response to change:

- Status – relative importance to others
- Certainty – ability to predict the future
- Autonomy – sense of control
- Relatedness – sense of safety with others
- Fairness – perception of equitable treatment

When people pivot, they often experience threat in at least three of these areas.

Leaving a role? Status and certainty plummet. Starting something alone? Relatedness and autonomy are threatened. Trying to change within a toxic system? Fairness becomes a psychological trigger.

That's why even "positive" pivots can feel destabilizing. The nervous system doesn't measure change by ambition—it measures change by risk.

The *Pivot Quotient* ™ redefines resilience as the ability to move through disruption while consciously recalibrating identity, safety, and autonomy.

It's trauma-informed transformation.

Narrative Healing: When the Brain Meets the Story

Here's where neuroscience and narrative collide.

Studies show that storytelling reduces activity in the amygdala (associated with fear) and increases oxytocin production (associated with empathy and connection) (Zak, 2015). When we give language to our lived experiences, we reduce physiological stress and increase resilience.

This is why your pivot story matters.

Not the polished version. The raw one. The version with doubt and detours and the moment you almost gave up.

Because when you narrate your shift with truth, your brain doesn't just remember—it reorganizes.

The hippocampus encodes new meaning. The default mode network lights up. Your sense of self is re-authored.

And that's not poetry. That's neuroscience.

Applied *P.I.V.O.T*™. in the Brain

Let's walk through the *P.I.V.O.T.*™ framework through the lens of brain science:

- Pause – Engages the parasympathetic nervous system, lowers cortisol, and creates the space for reflective thinking.
- Identify – Activates the anterior cingulate cortex and prefrontal regions responsible for self-awareness and perspective-taking.
- Validate – Calms the amygdala through emotional labeling and promotes emotion regulation via the ventromedial prefrontal cortex.
- Own – Reinforces agency by shifting activation to the brain's reward circuitry, especially when ownership leads to aligned action.
- Take Action – Triggers dopamine release through goal-oriented behavior and builds confidence through successful micro-decisions.

You're not just practicing resilience. You're remodeling your mind.

Real-Life Parallel: From Correction to Calibration

When I left the correctional system, my pivot wasn't just logistical—it was neurological.

I had to learn to regulate my nervous system after years of hypervigilance.

I had to mourn the identity that was rooted in bureaucracy and burnout.

I had to practice embodiment: morning walks, long breaths, water instead of worry.

The first time I spoke about trauma in a boardroom, my hands shook—not because I was unprepared, but because I was no longer dissociating. I was present. Fully. And that presence changed how the room responded.

Pivoting isn't a speech. It's a synaptic rewrite.

Resolution: Practice the Pivot Rehearsal

Here's a practical framework I call *Pivot Rehearsal*—designed to create embodied safety before bold steps:

1. Regulate – Pause. Breathe. Center yourself. (Safety first.)
2. Rehearse – Say the next action aloud. Picture it. What comes up?
3. Root – Anchor in a value: "Why does this matter to me or someone I love?"
4. Repeat – Neuroplasticity thrives on repetition. Build the new default.

And then? You move.

Not perfectly. But powerfully.

Final Word: Your Brain Was Built for This

There's a myth that trauma makes us broken. But what if it actually made us brilliant?

What if the parts of your brain that adapted to pain are now the parts helping you navigate reinvention?

What if your pivot isn't a rebellion—but a remembering?

You are not too late.
You are not too damaged.
You are not too far behind.

You are, in fact, exactly where your biology and your story have agreed to meet.

And every step forward?
Is a sacred neurological revolution.

Chapter Takeaways

- Neuroscience proves that change is not just possible—it's physiological. Your brain can be rewired.
- Trauma, identity disruption, and the SCARF model all shape how we pivot under pressure.

THE SCIENCE OF THE PIVOT

Mirror Moment™

Your space to reflect, reveal, and realign.

The Science of the Pivot (Tools in Action)
Comparative PQ Rubric Analysis

Now that you've explored these cases individually, here's how they score side-by-side on the PQ Scoring Rubric:

Case	Pause	Identify	Validate	Own	Take Action	Total PQ
Zoom	5	5	5	4	5	24/25
J.Crew	2	2	1	2	2	9/25
DOC	1	2	1	2	1	7/25

Key Insight:

Zoom exemplifies *High PQ™*—resilient, adaptive, and agile. J.Crew and DOC demonstrate what happens when organizations lack the ability to pause, identify, validate, own, and take action in alignment with their core values and external demands.

Your Turn – PQ Scoring Exercise:

1. Score your own organization or team using the PQ rubric.
2. Identify your weakest pillar (Pause, Identify, Validate, Own, or Take Action).
3. Create one micro-action for the next thirty days to strengthen that pillar.

Pro Tip: Revisit the PQ rubric quarterly to track your organization's resilience evolution.

Chapter 13

PIVOT QUOTIENT™: HOW WE NOW MEASURE RESILIENCE

Unpopular Truth: Grit isn't always enough. What determines your longevity isn't just how much you can endure—but how intelligently you adapt.

Before we turn the page and step fully into the framework, let's take a breath together. In Chapter 9, we talked about bounce-back speed—not as a feel-good phrase, but as a critical measure of leadership durability. We framed resilience as a reflex, not a résumé skill. Then, in Chapter 9.5, we answered the critics. We defended the Pivot Quotient™ *as a legitimate, scalable metric—one built not just from theory but from lived leadership, cultural urgency, and academic backbone.*

Now we pivot again—from concept to container.

This chapter is the blueprint. The tool. The mirror and the map.

Because legacy is not built on charisma. It's built on codified systems that can outlive your presence and outwork your emotions. The *Pivot Quotient*™ is that system.

If IQ tells us what you know.
And EQ tells us how you relate.
Then PQ tells us how you recover, realign, and rise—again and again.

This is where we stop reacting and start architecting. This is where you stop wondering if you're ready—and start measuring why you already are.

Welcome to Chapter 13.

Let's build.

There's a new currency in leadership, legacy, and life. It's not IQ. Not EQ. Not your GPA, your resume, or your highlight reel. It's your *Pivot Quotient*™ (PQ)—the measure of how well you shift under pressure, evolve through adversity, and rise through recalibration.

We live in an age where change is constant, uncertainty is normalized, and burnout is baked into systems that demand performance over presence. The ones who thrive aren't the ones who know the most—they're the ones who know how to move through the unknown.

PQ is your ability to process internalized vulnerability into optimal transformation. It's not just about surviving chaos—it's about converting chaos into capacity.

Defining the *Pivot Quotient*™

Pivot Quotient™ (PQ) is the measurable synthesis of adaptability, self-awareness, value-centered decision-making, and emotional agility. Where IQ asks, "What do you know?" and EQ asks, "How do you relate?"—PQ asks, "How do you evolve?"

PQ captures five core dimensions:
1. P – Pause with Intention: Can you slow down long enough to hear the deeper call within disruption?
2. I – Identify the Invitation: Do you recognize patterns that reveal who you're becoming?
3. V – Validate Your Truth: Can you honor your emotions without becoming hostage to them?
4. O – Own the Outcome: Do you take aligned action, regardless of the circumstances you didn't choose?
5. T – Take Strategic Action: Do you move without waiting for perfection or permission?

High PQ™ individuals don't just bounce back—they bounce forward.

Why We Need a New Resilience Metric

PQ isn't only a response to disruption. It's a reflection of discernment. It measures not just how we recover—but how wisely we choose when it's time to evolve, even without a crisis pushing us.

Traditional resilience measures are rooted in endurance. They ask: *How much can you take?*

PQ asks: *How intelligently can you shift when the stakes are high, the plan has failed, and the timeline is unclear?*

In an era of compounding trauma, public grief, pandemics, layoffs, and burnout, endurance is no longer enough. We need resilient intelligence—the capacity to pivot with strategy, story, and soul.

The *Pivot Quotient™* is for anyone who:

- Leads a team through constant disruption
- Coaches athletes navigating mental health
- Supports students in systems not built for their brilliance
- Parents children with complex needs
- Builds businesses from broken blueprints
- Refuses to make peace with systems that weren't made for them

Tools to Assess and Build Your PQ

Here are three frameworks to assess and develop *Pivot Quotient™* in yourself and your organization:

1. The *PQ Inventory™* (Self-Assessment Tool)

This diagnostic helps individuals assess their pivot literacy. It evaluates:

- Emotional Regulation Under Pressure (ERUPT)
- Speed of Cognitive Reframing (SCR)
- Identity Differentiation Index (IDI)
- Purposeful Adaptation Capacity (PAC)

Sample prompt: *When faced with rejection, do I recalibrate within hours, days, or months? What story do I tell myself in the meantime?*

2. The *Team Shift Spectrum*™

Used by leaders, educators, and athletic coaches to assess collective resilience:

- Do we encourage experimentation or punish mistakes?
- Do we pivot or panic when the playbook fails?
- Are debriefs rooted in blame or learning?

High PQ™ teams prioritize recovery, feedback loops, and psychological safety.

3. The *Pivot Quotient Playbook*™ *(P.Q.P.)*

For entrepreneurs, managers, and creatives building from scratch:

- Daily micro-adjustments tracked over time
- Weekly PQ "check-ins" to document shifts in clarity, energy, values, and action
- Pre-mortem reflection questions: "What might cause us to need a pivot mid-launch? Are we prepared to evolve on the fly?"

Case Studies Across Sectors

✦ Healthcare: The Nurse Who Became a Tech CEO

Devon, an ICU nurse, became burned out during COVID. Instead of leaving medicine altogether, she launched a digital platform to support frontline workers. Her *Pivot Quotient*™ showed up in her ability to identify exhaustion as data, not failure.

✦ Education: The Principal Who Rewrote the Discipline Model

James, a high school principal in an underserved district, pivoted from punitive models to restorative circles after seeing student suspension rates skyrocket. His team's PQ grew as they built culture before curriculum.

✦ Entrepreneurship: The Coach Who Lost Her Voice—Then Found Her Platform

Maya, a vocal coach, developed vocal nodules and had to cancel all gigs. That silence became sacred. She launched a course on "Speaking with Soul" and tripled her impact. Her PQ lay in her ability to let grief be her greatest guide.

✦ Athletics: The Player Who Sat Out to Stand Taller

Simone Biles didn't compete for the gold. She competed for her well-being. And in doing so, she showed the world that protecting your peace is a pivot worth celebrating.

These aren't stories of luck. They're stories of legacy. They remind us that *Pivot Quotient*™ is not about perfection—it's about permission.

As I continue to refine the *Pivot Quotient*™, it has become clear that resilience exists on a spectrum. From *Reactive PQ*™, where pivots are born of survival, to *Regenerative PQ*™, where pivots are sourced from intention—this spectrum helps leaders and learners alike identify where they are, and where they're growing toward.

Why Critics Might Push Back—And Why They're Missing the Point

Some may say PQ is just another personal development buzzword. That it over-intellectualizes what people have always done: adapt.

But here's the truth:

- PQ provides language for legacy. Language we can name; language we can nurture.
- PQ is intersectional. It accounts for systemic barriers, emotional labor, and cultural context.
- PQ is measurable and actionable. It's not fluff. It's a framework grounded in neuroscience, narrative therapy, organizational psychology, and qualitative lived experience.
- PQ decentralizes perfection. It elevates micro-movements, not big leaps.

Your Turn: Calculate Your PQ

Ask yourself:

- What was my last major disruption? What did I *learn*, *shift*, or *shed* as a result?
- What limiting belief am I still hosting instead of healing?
- Where am I resisting the pivot because it doesn't match my original plan?
- Who are my "Shift Circle" people—the ones who help me evolve without ego?

Now complete this prompt:
"My Pivot Quotient™ *rises when I…"*

Say it out loud. Then move like you believe it.

Final Word: Pivot Is the New Power

Let this be clear: The *Pivot Quotient*™ is not about bounce-back height. It's about bounce-back speed, strategy, and soul.

It's the quiet courage to listen deeper. The permission to evolve publicly. The refusal to make stagnation sacred. The sacred dance between discomfort and destiny.

In a world obsessed with visibility, PQ asks you to become fluent in internal agility. Because the greatest leaders of the future won't just be those who perform well—they'll be those who pivot wisely.

So, honor your adaptability. Track your bounce. Lead your legacy.

Because resilience isn't the destination. It's the response.

And *Pivot Quotient*™?

It's the new compass.

Chapter Takeaways

- A *High PQ*™ life is not just reactive—it's proactive. It builds bounce-back muscles before life requires them.
- Recovery, reflection, and recalibration are your new rituals—not just when things go wrong, but so they go right.

Mirror Moment™

Your space to reflect, reveal, and realign.

Chapter 14

REWRITING THE FUTURE — FAITH, LEGACY, AND THE COURAGE TO IMAGINE BEYOND

Unpopular Truth: The future doesn't just arrive. It is authored.

There comes a moment when you realize your pivot is more than personal—it's generational. The decisions you make, the stories you reclaim, the boldness with which you move—they aren't only changing your life. They're reshaping what's possible for everyone connected to your name.

This chapter isn't just about shifting goals. It's about shifting gravity. It's about becoming the kind of person whose presence bends time—pulling forward the dreams your ancestors never got to finish and launching blueprints for generations you'll never meet. That's not strategy. That's stewardship.

The Future Isn't a Place. It's a Posture.

We often treat the future like a distant horizon, something we hope to reach if we can hustle hard enough or live long enough. But what if the future isn't something we step into—it's something we become?

You don't just prepare for the future. You shape it—through your choices, your courage, your pivots. Faith isn't the absence of uncertainty; it's the audacity to move when the map doesn't exist. And legacy isn't what you leave behind; it's what you plant and protect while you're here.

Beyond the Timeline: The *Nonlinear Legacy Model*™

Legacy isn't linear. It doesn't follow predictable paths. It loops. It evolves. It doubles back to heal what was broken before. That's the soul of *Nonlinear Legacy Building*™—a concept born from honoring both ancestry and agency.

Your pivot might not make sense to others. It may not look strategic. But some shifts aren't for applause. They're for alignment. They may disrupt expectations, but they activate legacy.

Every time you say, "This stops with me," or "This begins with me," you're authoring futures—on purpose.

The Universal Invitation: Prophetic Resilience

You don't need to belong to one faith tradition to understand the necessity of belief. We all, at some point, must act on things we cannot yet prove. That's prophetic resilience: the choice to move as if the outcome is already promised. To build with no blueprint. To persist when progress isn't visible.

Whether you're a tech entrepreneur in Detroit, a single father in Nairobi, or a teacher rebuilding after burnout—your vision is valid. Your imagination is radical. And your willingness to act on that vision is what makes it real.

This isn't a chapter about religion. It's about the sacred responsibility of vision.

Pivoting as a Cultural Architect

In every system—family, education, business, government—someone is shaping culture. And, if you're reading this book, chances are … that someone is you.

You're not just reacting to your circumstances. You're redefining the climate in which others will breathe, build, and belong. That's not ego—it's evidence of impact. Every choice you make to show up differently becomes architecture. It builds the unseen structure that future generations will stand on.

Ask yourself:

- What dysfunction am I no longer available to normalize?
- What truth am I finally ready to speak—even if my voice shakes?
- What kind of future deserves my labor, my loyalty, and my leadership?

Real-World Legacy Builders

Kiran, a second-generation immigrant and software developer, pivoted out of Big Tech to build an AI literacy program for underserved youth. "I realized I was contributing to systems that didn't include my community," he said. "So, I built one that did."

Elena, a veteran and mother of three, started a cooperative farm that employs formerly incarcerated women. "I didn't just want to feed bodies. I wanted to nourish possibility."

Malik, a recovering addict, now mentors teenage boys in South Florida through basketball and poetry. "I pivoted not because I was ready," he says, "but because I was tired of watching kids drown in the same waters I nearly did."

These aren't just stories. They're signals. They're proof that when we pivot with purpose, we shift more than circumstances—we shift systems.

The *P.I.V.O.T.*™ Framework as Legacy Engine

Let's land this in action. The *P.I.V.O.T.*™ framework is more than a personal growth tool. It's an intergenerational mechanism. A sacred structure for reimagining what's possible across time and identity.

- **Pause** – Create quiet space to hear what legacy is calling you to birth or break.

- **Identify** – Trace the generational patterns you've inherited. Decide which ones end with you.
- **Validate** – Acknowledge the full spectrum of your lineage—both the burdens and the brilliance.
- **Own** – Step into your authority. You don't need a title to leave an impact.
- **Take Action** – Move now. Move even when the future isn't fully visible. The act of moving is what makes it visible.

Mirror Moment™

Reflect on this question: *What would it mean for my pivot to become someone else's permission slip?*

Write it. Speak it. Walk it out.

A New Kind of Ancestry

You are not just someone's child—you are someone's ancestor.

And that should mean something.

Because whether you come from royalty or rubble, brilliance or brokenness, your legacy is yours to define. You don't have to repeat what you inherited. You don't have to normalize what harmed you. You don't have to shrink to survive.

You can pivot on purpose. You can plant something permanent in a world obsessed with the temporary.

You can become the ancestor your descendants will thank out loud.

Final Word: Shift the Future Anyway

The future will not remember your perfection. It will remember your pivot. It will echo your courage.

So, move like your grandchild is watching. Lead like the world you want already exists. Build like your ancestors are whispering, "Keep going."

And when fear tries to convince you it's too soon, too risky, or too bold—remember this:

You were born for this.

Now shift.

Chapter Takeaways

- Every pivot has the power to redeem the past and redesign the future.
- Faith isn't just about belief—it's about building what hasn't been seen yet, for those who haven't yet arrived.

You've made it through the framework—but the real journey starts now. You're not just shifting—you're shaping. You're not just surviving—you're seeding the future. Now go—live it, lead it, leave a legacy with every pivot.

Just remember, legacy isn't just what we leave—it's what we systematize. *High PQ*™ is already becoming a generational blueprint, with the tools, matrix, and pivot archetypes serving as the infrastructure for transformational leadership in every sector.

Mirror Moment™

Your space to reflect, reveal, and realign.

Chapter 15

VOICES THAT LAID THE GROUNDWORK — AND WHY I CHOSE TO BUILD MY OWN BLUEPRINT

Unpopular Truth: Respecting the greats doesn't mean repeating them—sometimes the boldest act of legacy is outgrowing the blueprint you were taught to revere.

We all stand on the shoulders of someone—mentors we've never met, teachers we didn't know we needed, voices that rose just high enough for us to hear them across time. For me, honoring the voices that came before isn't about echoing their words—it's about activating their courage and advancing the conversation. Reverence doesn't mean restriction. It means recognizing the seeds that were sown and being bold enough to grow something new.

I've spent years listening, learning, unlearning, and ultimately building a system that reflects *not just what I've read*, but *what I've lived.* This chapter is both a bow and a boundary—a nod to the trailblazers, and a clear pivot into my own lane.

Tony Robbins taught millions that "where focus goes, energy flows." He introduced the idea that internal shifts ignite external results. But *High PQ*™ asks: *What if your focus has been fractured by identity, trauma, or systemic invisibility?* The *Pivot Quotient*™ doesn't just redirect your focus—it *reclaims* it.

Jim Rohn (1994) told us, "Discipline is the bridge between goals and accomplishment." His wisdom still echoes. But what he didn't say was that some of us never got the blueprint for the bridge. The *Micro-Decision Tracker*™, born from the *P.I.V.O.T.*™ framework, lays every brick—from self-awareness to radical ownership.

Viktor Frankl (2006) showed us that between stimulus and response lies our power to choose. His insights were profound. But when survival is your baseline, choice feels like a privilege. The *Pause Map*™ helps people move from survival to strategy—because reclaiming your breath *is* reclaiming your power.

Audre Lorde (1988) reminded us that "self-care is not self-indulgence, it is self-preservation." But preservation isn't enough for those of us called to build legacies. In the world of *High PQ*™, we pivot not only to heal—but to *construct new systems of flourishing*.

bell hooks (2000) told us that love is a political act. That healing must happen in community. Her words gave language to what many of us already felt. But language is only the beginning. The *Freedom to Flourish*™ system is a direct descendant of her truth—translating love into *infrastructure*.

Carol Dweck (2006) introduced the world to the power of growth mindset—an idea that reshaped education and leadership forever. But mindset alone is insufficient without maps. The *Pivot Quotient*™, is mindset *in motion*, guided by tools that reflect lived complexity, cultural nuance, and embodied transformation.

Stephen Covey (1989) taught us to lead from principle, from the inside out. His habits changed lives. *High PQ*™ pushes that concept into new territory: leadership forged not only by principle, but by pivots—by choosing courage when clarity isn't guaranteed.

These are the voices that whispered to me through pages, lectures, interviews, and silent nights of reckoning. They cracked something open. But what poured out wasn't replication—it was revelation. My frameworks weren't written in ivory towers. They were birthed in hospital rooms, prison systems, corporate boardrooms, and mothering through midnight crises.

They whispered freedom.
I built a system for it.

High PQ™ didn't materialize in a vacuum—it was born in the spaces between reverence and resistance, between what was offered and what was still missing. The voices that laid the groundwork gave us access, but it's up to us to build something worthy of the moment we're living in. *You* are now part of that evolution. This is no longer about the wisdom of others—it's about the wisdom awakening in *you*. And that's where we turn next: to the final charge, the invitation, the undeniable truth.

Your pivot story is not just personal. It's prophetic.

Chapter Takeaways

- **Innovation doesn't betray tradition—it fulfills it.** Honoring the trailblazers who came before us is not about mimicry; it's about continuation with elevation. *High PQ*™ is the next chapter in a long lineage of resilience, reinvention, and radical truth-telling. When you build your own blueprint, you don't abandon their work—you extend their vision.
- **The truest legacy is not repeating greatness but responding to what your generation uniquely needs.** Every quote, every framework, every system I've created was born not just from inspiration—but from lived urgency. Your story deserves a system rooted in *now*, not nostalgia. The *Pivot Quotient*™ is what happens when wisdom meets today's complexity.

Mirror Moment™

Your space to reflect, reveal, and realign.

Chapter 16

PREVIEW WHAT'S NEXT

Unpopular Truth: Resilience has never been an individual achievement—it has always been an ecosystem, and pretending otherwise is why so many leaders, teams, and cultures collapse.

This book is the foundation. But High PQ™ *is already expanding into a full ecosystem—complete with assessment tools, archetypes, and organizational models that quantify what's often left unseen.* High PQ™ 2.0 *is already in motion.*

As we stand at the edge of what's next, *High PQ™ 2.0* ushers in a new frontier—one where resilience is no longer an isolated trait, but an integrated system. This isn't about bouncing back alone. This is about building forward—together.

What if your pivot wasn't just a moment—but a mechanism?

In *The Ecosystem Era*, we move beyond individual reinvention and into collective transformation. We explore the ripple effects of PQ in families, teams, institutions, and cultures. We examine how organizational pivots require emotional fluency. How communities regenerate when legacy is nonlinear. How teams rise when psychological safety, adaptive leadership, and narrative intelligence converge.

What follows is a window into what's next:

- The ***PQ Multiplier Effect*** ™: How one person's pivot can shift entire systems.
- The ***Resilience Constellation*** ™: Mapping interdependent support structures.
- The **Leadership Archetypes of *High PQ* ™ Teams**.
- And the dawn of ***PQ-Driven Culture Design*** ™: Where strategy meets soul.

High PQ ™ *2.0* is not just a workbook or a workshop. It's a way of seeing, building, and leading. It's data-backed, spirit-driven, and designed for the future of work, wellbeing, and the world.

Because the next evolution of leadership isn't about managing people through change.
It's about *activating ecosystems that are built to adapt.*
You were never meant to pivot in isolation.
You were meant to become the ecosystem your lineage prayed for.

The next pivot of this work includes the *PQ Matrix* ™, Resilience Archetypes, and scalable assessments for teams and institutions. *High PQ* ™ *2.0* isn't just a theory—it's a toolkit for legacy-driven leadership, equity, and reinvention.

This is the era of *High PQ™*. And it's only just begun.

Figure 16.1 – *High PQ™ 2.0:* Ecosystem Era.

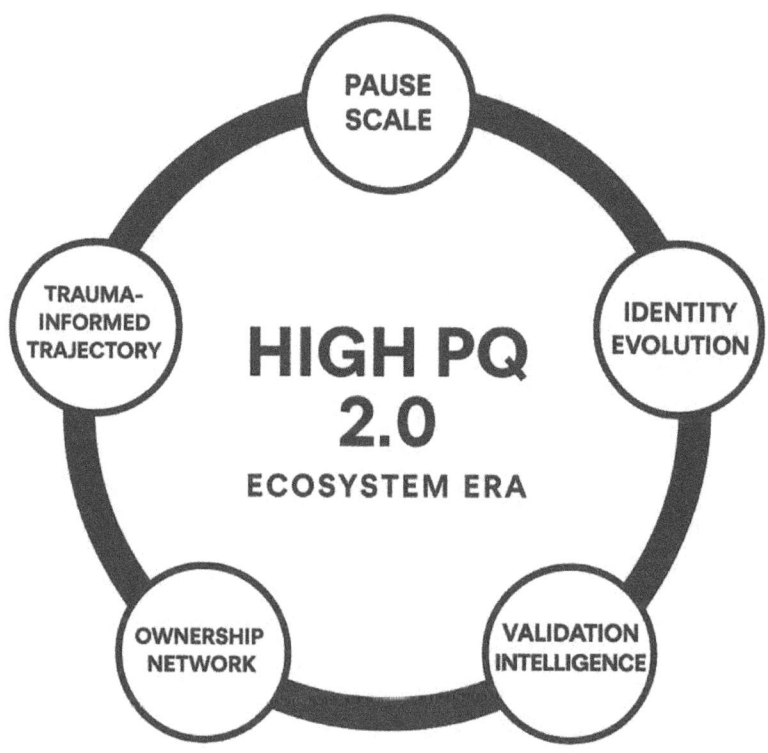

Figure 16.1 The High PQ™: *Ecosystem Era represents a dynamic, interconnected framework where tools, teachings, and transformational experiences converge—empowering individuals, teams, and institutions to pivot with precision, build resilient cultures, and embed legacy into every decision across personal, professional, and generational domains.*

Conclusion

The Pivot That Changed Everything

There are books that educate, others that inspire—and then there are books like this one, born not from concept but from conviction. *High PQ™: The P.I.V.O.T. Quotient That Changes Everything* is more than a framework—it's a lifeline. A mirror. A match. A movement.

High PQ™ is a resilience operating system.

A way of thinking, responding, and rebuilding that belongs in boardrooms, classrooms, prisons, and policies.

The *P.I.V.O.T.™* framework may be personal, but its reach is systemic.

Writing this was no easy feat. It required excavating truths I'd buried, naming fears I'd navigated in silence, and translating the rhythm of my resilience into language that could liberate others. This was not an intellectual exercise—it was a spiritual pilgrimage. I cried writing some of these chapters. I wrestled with doubt. I questioned whether the pain, the pivots, and the perseverance would translate into tools others could use. And yet, I knew I had to keep going.

Because someone needs this blueprint.
Someone needs permission.
Someone needs to know they aren't broken—they are building.

We started this book with a radical premise: that pivots are not detours. They are directions. That success isn't linear, and that leadership isn't reserved for the chosen few—it's forged in disruption, recovery, and truth-telling. Every chapter in this book reflects a layer of the *P.I.V.O.T.™* framework:

- **Pause** taught us that stillness isn't weakness—it's strategy.

- **Identify** reminded us that naming the loss is the first step toward legacy.
- **Validate** showed us that honoring our emotions is a radical act of wholeness.
- **Own** gave us permission to claim our power without apology.
- **Take Action** dared us to move without waiting for the world to catch up.

And then we kept building. We introduced the *Pivot Quotient*™—a resilience metric for those who lead from the ashes, rise with wisdom, and land with clarity. We debunked the myth of linear growth, emphasized the science behind the shift, and honored the sacred work of those rewriting the future—not just for themselves, but for generations.

This wasn't just a book. It was a reckoning.
And now, it's your turn.

It's your turn to walk into the next chapter of your life with full authority and no apology. It's your turn to apply the tools, track your micro-decisions, and map your own transformation.
It's your turn to build a life you don't need permission to live.

Whether you're pivoting out of grief, out of burnout, out of disillusionment—or into something more aligned, more expansive, more honest—you have what you need.

You are not behind. You are not broken.
You are being rerouted—on purpose.

Let this be your declaration: I do not pivot because I failed. I pivot because I'm evolving. Because I'm discerning. Because I'm done waiting.

And when fear rises, let these words settle you:

You are not the mistake. You are the miracle in motion.
You are not too much. You are exactly enough for the mission ahead.
You are not here to perform. You are here to become.

God's divine choreography never wastes a step. Every twist, every detour, every delayed "yes" has prepared you for this moment.

So, take a deep breath.

Turn the page on what no longer fits.

And pivot—boldly, unapologetically, powerfully.

Because *Shift Happens*. And now, you're ready for it.

Welcome to your next chapter. Let's rise.

Acknowledgments

The Grace Behind the Grit

To every person who's been told you're "too loud," "too bold," "too much"—and chose to become *even more*—this is for you. This is your fire, your reflection, your home.

My daughter, Kendall, the heartbeat behind every page: your diagnosis did not break me—it built me. You taught me what no degree ever could: resilience is not a theory; it's a lifestyle. Your courage rewrote my calling. Your laughter reminded me to live. You are my greatest *why*.

My parents—Maureen and Cleveland—thank you for the kind of love that steadied me when life tried to shake me. Your work ethic, sacrifice, and quiet strength are stitched into my DNA. Every prayer you whispered, every boundary you held, every story you shared planted seeds of legacy that I now tend with pride.

To the women who pivoted while bleeding. Who led without applause. Who questioned everything and moved anyway. This book is not just for you—it is *about* you. You are the unsung architects of change, and this framework carries your fingerprint.

To the ones who saw me before I fully saw myself—mentors, teachers, pastors, professors, coaches, and truth-tellers—you fanned flames I once thought were smoke. You reminded me that I did not need a crown to rule, a platform to speak, or a map to move.

To the men who have held space, not out of pity but partnership—thank you for amplifying rather than overshadowing. To the fathers, brothers, sons, and co-conspirators of liberation—your courage to evolve matters here, too.

My *Freedom to Flourish*™ and Civilian Corrections Academy family—your trust in the frameworks born from my journey has carried them beyond the page. Thank you for daring to grow with me. Thank you for choosing to grow alongside me.

My soul circle, my real ones, the ones who remind me who I am when the world gets noisy—you are my safe place to land and leap.

My executive editors, creative collaborators, and fellow thought leaders—thank you for helping me sculpt my chaos into clarity. Your fingerprints are on these pages.

To every reader who cracked this book open in search of *something*—direction, peace, purpose, fire—I want you to know: this is more than words. It's a mirror. A match. A movement. You don't need permission to shift. You just need truth. Welcome home.

And to God—thank You for being the ultimate strategist. Thank You for the doors You closed, the delays You orchestrated, and the divine detours that shaped me into the woman who could not just *write* this message—but *embody* it.

Every pivot was planned. Every scar was sacred. Every yes, holy.

This isn't just a thank you. It's a hand extended back.

Let's rise.

References

Ajzen, Icek. 1991. "The Theory of Planned Behavior." *Organizational Behavior and Human Decision Processes* 50 (2): 179–211. https://doi.org/10.1016/0749-5978(91)90020-T.

Bandura, Albert. 1997. *Self-Efficacy: The Exercise of Control.* New York: W. H. Freeman.

Baumeister, Roy F., Ellen Bratslavsky, Mark Muraven, and Dianne M. Tice. 1998. "Ego Depletion: Is the Active Self a Limited Resource?" *Journal of Personality and Social Psychology* 74 (5): 1252–65. https://doi.org/10.1037/0022-3514.74.5.1252.

Beck, Aaron T. 1976. *Cognitive Therapy and the Emotional Disorders.* New York: International Universities Press.

Bowen, Murray. 1978. *Family Therapy in Clinical Practice.* New York: Jason Aronson.

Collins, Patricia Hill. 2000. *Black Feminist Thought: Knowledge, Consciousness, and the Politics of Empowerment.* 2nd ed. New York: Routledge.

Covey, Stephen R. 1989. *The 7 Habits of Highly Effective People: Powerful Lessons in Personal Change.* New York: Free Press.

Crenshaw, Kimberlé. 1991. "Mapping the Margins: Intersectionality, Identity Politics, and Violence against Women of Color." *Stanford Law Review* 43 (6): 1241–99. https://doi.org/10.2307/1229039.

David, Susan. 2016. *Emotional Agility: Get Unstuck, Embrace Change, and Thrive in Work and Life.* New York: Avery.

Dery, Mark. 1994. "Black to the Future: Interviews with Samuel R. Delany, Greg Tate, and Tricia Rose." In *Flame Wars: The Discourse of Cyberculture*, edited by Mark Dery, 179–222. Durham, NC: Duke University Press.

Duckworth, Angela L., Christopher Peterson, Michael D. Matthews, and Dennis R. Kelly. 2007. "Grit: Perseverance and Passion for Long-Term Goals." *Journal of Personality and Social Psychology* 92 (6): 1087–1101. https://doi.org/10.1037/0022-3514.92.6.1087.

Dweck, Carol S. 2006. *Mindset: The New Psychology of Success.* New York: Random House.

Frankl, Viktor E. 2006. *Man's Search for Meaning.* Translated by Ilse Lasch. Boston: Beacon Press. (Originally published 1946.)

Goleman, Daniel. 1995. *Emotional Intelligence: Why It Can Matter More than IQ.* New York: Bantam Books.

hooks, bell. 2000. *All About Love: New Visions.* New York: William Morrow.

Immordino-Yang, Mary Helen, Joanna A. Christodoulou, and Vanessa Singh. 2012. "Rest Is Not Idleness: Implications of the Brain's Default Mode for Human Development and Education." *Perspectives on Psychological Science* 7 (4): 352–64. https://doi.org/10.1177/1745691612447308.

Johnson, Spencer. 1998. *Who Moved My Cheese? An Amazing Way to Deal with Change in Your Work and in Your Life.* New York: G. P. Putnam's Sons.

Kanter, Rosabeth Moss. 1979. "Power Failure in Management Circuits." *Harvard Business Review* 57 (4, July–August): 65–75.

Linehan, Marsha M. 1993. *Cognitive-Behavioral Treatment of Borderline Personality Disorder.* New York: Guilford Press.

Lorde, Audre. 1988. *A Burst of Light: Essays.* Ithaca, NY: Firebrand Books.

Maslow, Abraham H. 1943. "A Theory of Human Motivation." *Psychological Review* 50 (4): 370–96. https://doi.org/10.1037/h0054346.

McAdams, Dan P. 2001. "The Psychology of Life Stories." *Review of General Psychology* 5 (2): 100–22. https://doi.org/10.1037/1089-2680.5.2.100.

Pychyl, Timothy A. 2013. *Solving the Procrastination Puzzle: A Concise Guide to Strategies for Change.* New York: TarcherPerigee.

Rohn, Jim. 1994. *The Treasury of Quotes.* Dallas: Jim Rohn International.

Rotter, Julian B. 1966. "Generalized Expectancies for Internal versus External Control of Reinforcement." *Psychological Monographs: General and Applied* 80 (1): 1–28. https://doi.org/10.1037/h0092976.

Shenk, Chad, and Alan E. Fruzzetti. 2011. "The Impact of Validating and Invalidating Responses on Emotional Reactivity." *Journal of Social and Clinical Psychology* 30 (2): 163–83. https://doi.org/10.1521/jscp.2011.30.2.163.

Stryker, Sheldon, and Peter J. Burke. 2000. "The Past, Present, and Future of an Identity Theory." *Social Psychology Quarterly* 63 (4): 284–97. https://doi.org/10.2307/2695840.

Tedeschi, Richard G., and Lawrence G. Calhoun. 2004. "Posttraumatic Growth: Conceptual Foundations and Empirical Evidence." *Psychological Inquiry* 15 (1): 1–18. https://doi.org/10.1207/s15327965pli1501_01.

Young, Valerie. 2011. *The Secret Thoughts of Successful Women: Why Capable People Suffer from the Impostor Syndrome and How to Thrive in Spite of It.* New York: Crown Publishing Group.

Appendix A

Legacy Lineage: The Evolution That Led to High PQ™

> "Every system has a season. This one—*is mine.*"
> — Constantine J. Alleyne

The *Pivot Quotient*™ system didn't appear from thin air. It is the product of decades of evolution—from therapeutic insight and motivational theory to liberation psychology and radical reinvention. This Legacy Lineage Timeline honors the architects whose voices cracked something open in me—and sets the stage for what I was uniquely born to build. This is more than a map of influence. It is proof that every system has a season … and this one—*is mine.*

The Lineage of Legacy: 1940s–2020s

Era	Legacy Thinker	Quote	Legacy Contribution → *High PQ*™ Advancement
1940s–50s	Viktor Frankl	"When we are no longer able to change a situation, we are challenged to change ourselves."	Introduced meaning as a path to healing → *High PQ's Pause Map*™ creates space for intentional response.
1970s–80s	bell hooks (lowercase)	"I will not have my life narrowed down. I will not bow down to somebody else's whim or to someone else's ignorance."	Centered love and healing as liberation → *Freedom to Flourish*™ builds loving infrastructure for legacy.

1980s–90s	Jim Rohn	*"Discipline is the bridge between goals and accomplishment."*	Advocated daily mastery → *High PQ's Micro-Decision Tracker*™ builds disciplined momentum.
1990s–2000s	Tony Robbins	*"It is in your moments of decision that your destiny is shaped."*	Popularized internal transformation → *High PQ's Inner Voice Rewrite*™ makes identity shifts measurable.
2000s–2010s	Brené Brown	*"Vulnerability is not weakness; it's our greatest measure of courage."*	Normalized emotional exposure → *High PQ's P.I.V.O.T.*™ framework turns vulnerability into reinvention.
2010s–2020s	Carol Dweck	*"Becoming is better than being."*	Created growth mindset theory → *High PQ's Pivot Quotient*™ operationalizes growth in real time.

The Blueprint Builder Emerges

Now	Constantine J. Alleyne	*"They whispered freedom. I built a system for it."*	Creator of the *P.I.V.O.T.*™ framework, *Pivot Quotient*™, and *Freedom to Flourish*™. Reimagined resilience as a measurable, identity-rooted, culturally relevant pathway to legacy. Her work is the convergence of story, strategy, neuroscience, and soul.

PREVIEW WHAT'S NEXT

Mirror Moment™:

*Which of these legacy voices speaks most deeply to your own pivot story—
and how might you honor them by building your own blueprint?*

www.ingramcontent.com/pod-product-compliance
Lightning Source LLC
Chambersburg PA
CBHW080413170426
43194CB00015B/2802